Real Time Devotionals: Book of John Volume 1

By Joe Anderson

Copyright ©2024 by Joe Anderson

For more information visit truthbursts.com

Front Cover Design: Teal Rose Design Studios

Interior Design: Robert Sweesy, Endurance Press

Print ISBN: 978-1-7363842-9-9

Published by Endurance Press

I dedicate this effort to primarily to My Lord and Savior Jesus Christ. He is the reason I experience true vibrancy in this life that is beyond compare! I also write in the spirit of the witness my mom, Charlene Duke Anderson (in heaven now), showed in her ministry to the poor, the hurting, the orphans, and the widows at the San Jose Rescue Mission. Her faithfulness in trying times, while dying of cancer, propels me to speak of the Lord and Savior we both served/serve.

Forward

Book of John Devotionals
The Gospel of John is one of the most widely-read gospels in the Bible. It is written by one of Jesus' closest friends, the Apostle John. While Jesus was dying on the cross, it was the Apostle John who Jesus asked to take care of his mother going forward. It is fascinating to see how John brings out the passion and emotion involving Jesus' time here on earth.
It all starts with John 1:1-5:

In the beginning was the Word, and the Word was with God, and the Word was God. He was with God in the beginning. Through him all things were made; without him nothing was made that has been made. In him was life, and that life was the light of all mankind. The light shines in the darkness, and the darkness has not overcome it.

The Gospel of John states from the beginning that Jesus was with God at creation and made everything, he is God in the human form sent to earth, and the magnitude of the life in him is so great it acts as a light for all of mankind over all ages. Pretty powerful stuff!
Throughout the book, we find Jesus standing up for truth, healing, performing miracles, and teaching his disciples the way to follow God by living out "God's Way" in his life. In John 14:6 it says: "Jesus answered, 'I am the way, the truth, and the life. No one comes to the Father except through me.'"
As I have written these devotionals, I have tried to relate them to everyday life. You will find real-life stories, analogies, and comparisons to give some examples of how these

words apply to our current world. I have not shied away from controversial topics or people, but try to use examples I see in the world that apply to the passages I am studying.

It is my hope that not only will these devotionals encourage you, but they will also propel you on to a richer time studying God's Word and digging out the great nuggets of truth and wisdom therein.

Taking time to write down growth action steps and celebrate the progress you have made here are important steps to move from reading to implementing. We have provided space for this!

I hope you enjoy reading God's word and seeing it come alive more and more in your life! I am praying for you in advance for some great spiritual breakthroughs. GOD LOVES YOU MORE!

Day 1

John 1:1-3

In the beginning was the Word, and the Word was with God, and the Word was God. He was with God in the beginning. Through him all things were made; without him nothing was made that has been made.

The Word — The Gravity of it All

When I think of words and the many forms they take, these come to mind: terms of endearment, commands and words of caution, songs of joy and songs of trial, poetry, books, encouraging sayings or phrases. Words have so much they bring to our lives. In Jesus' time, Greeks used the word "logos" for "word", which had a little different meaning than our English "word" does today. It not only encompassed the spoken word but also the unspoken word in the mind — the reason.

When they applied it to the universe, the word "logos" meant the rational principle that governs all things. In contrast, the Jews used it to refer to the "Word of God" by which he created the world and governs it. The Word of God was connected to the law of God, and this law was the way for them to receive their eternal inheritance. They even believe that God's Word rested on his chest before he created the world. We see here John's deliberate mirroring of Genesis 1, when he said, "In the beginning". Jesus is identified as "The Word" later in John 1, as we shall see. So John basically is intertwining all of the related things surrounding God and his Word. If I understand the context under which "logos" (meaning word) was used, John was saying: Jesus is all of God's sayings, thoughts, and reason in one person. He is the personification of God's law. God's law and he are one. He was with God at creation, and he was God at creation. He partnered with God to create us. All of God's creations were made through him.

So I learn here that the Jesus who was born a man was ancient and full of truth and power. He created and sustained life. He was God's reason and mind on this earth. This is so mind-boggling to me. I really stand in awe here ... wondering HOW COULD THIS BE? How could this powerful, ancient creator come to earth as a poor baby and love such a sinner as me? How could Jesus stoop to such a low level to rescue me? He truly was the Servant King and the Merciful Creator. Thank you, Lord Jesus, for being The Word of God; not just philosophical ideas but a word of POWERFUL ACTION, who took risks to love and sacrifice for his loved ones. May I follow in your Servant Leadership ways.

TAKEAWAYS

_____

_____

_____

_____

_____

Day 2
John 1:4-5 (AMP)

In Him was life [and the power to bestow life], and the life was the Light of men. The Light shines on in the darkness, and the darkness did not understand it or overpower it or appropriate it or absorb it [and is unreceptive to it].

Light Ambassadors

Light in our world is a life-source. It is one of the most critical elements for our existence. So critical is light in supporting life, that God created it right after creating the heavens and the earth. We use light along with water to grow our food. During the COVID outbreaks, we found that light and its byproduct, Vitamin D, are very important in fighting off disease and illness. And light makes us happy and productive. It gives us confidence to run and take risks. Daylight is the time we shine.

Spiritually, just like the sun, the moon, campfires, and our lightbulbs provide light, Jesus provides light in our hearts. He does this by shining his goodness into our lives. By his light, I can be made new — cleansed and refreshed by the Holy Spirit. And once my heart is full of Jesus' light, I get to shine it into the lives of those around me. More time with Jesus and his light makes me more brilliant to those around me. And I become a better lover of people, as I look for ways to bless them. Many people are looking for meaning in this life. By following Jesus closely, I get to be his Light Ambassador to a lost world!!! "We are therefore Christ's ambassadors, as though God were making his appeal through us. We implore you on Christ's behalf: Be reconciled to God."

(II Corinthians 5:20) Reconciled to God and Jesus = Reconciled to The Light. Lord, help me to be reconciled to your light today and learn to shine brightly to others by first filling up with your light. Everything radiates when your light shines! It brings joy and breathes hope into the most devastating circumstances. Your light is life and I thank you for it.

TAKEAWAYS

_____

_____

_____

_____

_____

Day 3

John 1:6-8

There was a man sent from God whose name was John. He came as a witness to testify concerning that light, so that through him all might believe. He himself was not the light; he came only as a witness to the light.

Parallel verse:

Hebrews 12:1

Therefore, since we are surrounded by such a great cloud of witnesses, let us throw off everything that hinders and the sin that so easily entangles. And let us run with perseverance the race marked out for us,

The Witness

John's job was to be a witness. He was a witness to the light. In fact, it is very important to the Apostle John that we understand that John the Baptist was a witness to "the light". He says the same thing two different ways in succession. To find out about this light, we must go back to verse 4, where it says, "In him was life, and that life was the light of men." So the light that shines out of The Word (Jesus) is true life. The light is the manifestation of the true life within. Jesus equals life because he created life. Hebrews 1 also tells us he sustains life with his powerful word. So John was sent as a witness to the light, which is the outward manifestation of the light of men, the light of the world, Jesus Christ.

So what is an active witness? An active witness tells others about their experiences and interaction with the subject. John told people about his interactions with Jesus and about the light of life inside him.

There are at least two other important passages about witnesses in the New Testament. "[Jesus speaking] He said to them: 'It is not for you to know the times or dates the Father has set by his own authority. But you will receive power when the Holy Spirit comes on you; and you will be my witnesses in Jerusalem, and in all Judea and Samaria, and to the ends of the earth.'" (Acts 1:7-8)

And so we who are disciples and followers of Jesus are all called to be "witnesses". And the Hebrews 12 passage above refers to those who have gone before us and died as a crowd of witnesses, cheering us on in life. Being a witness is spiritually important. It is how John was described. It is how the Saints of old are described. What actions can I take in life to be described as a witness to Jesus? How do I become an active witness of the gospel? Lord, teach me to be focused on what truly matters in life and not the "fluff" and ambient noise of this world.

TAKEAWAYS

_____

_____

_____

_____

Day 4

John 1:9-13

The true light that gives light to everyone was coming into the world. He was in the world, and though the world was made through him, the world did not recognize him. He came to that which was his own, but his own did not receive him. Yet to all who did receive him, to those who believed in his name, he gave the right to become children of God— children born not of natural descent, nor of human decision or a husband's will, but born of God.

Will I Receive God's Gift?

As a parent, I understand that children do not always receive the gifts I give them well. Sometimes with joy, as a small child, they will get a gift for their birthday, and then play with it for a few weeks, only to become bored with it. As children grow older, parents will try and give them different kinds of gifts: connections for college references, introductions for jobs, teaching them to work hard, to be honest, or to value and save money. These connections and disciplines can be gifts too, but many times teenagers want to try out life on their own and will ignore or seemingly go in the opposite direction when these gifts are given.

Jesus being born was a gift to mankind. A few recognized it — the wise men, the shepherds, Elizabeth, Simeon — and they praised God and worshipped him. Most did not recognize him or receive him. He was a true light, and this light, if followed, gives life to all. But many would choose not to follow him, just like today. For the few that did follow, and do follow today, Jesus gives the right to be born of God and become his children. This is what it means to be "born again". Jesus talks more about this in John 3. So how will I choose to receive God's Gift — the light of Jesus — today? Will I allow it to breathe life into my weary bones? Lord, teach me to receive your good gifts each day. May your life be in my heart and teach me to shine it into the lives of others.

TAKEAWAYS

_____

_____

_____

_____

_____

Day 5

John 1:14-16

The Word became flesh and made his dwelling among us. We have seen his glory, the glory of the one and only Son, who came from the Father, full of grace and truth. (John testified concerning him. He cried out, saying, "This is the one I spoke about when I said, 'He who comes after me has surpassed me because he was before me.'") From the fullness of his grace we all have received one blessing after another.

Guides Through the Narrow Gate

Though I haven't been there, I have heard about how they take ships through the Panama Canal. It seems they have two roads on either side of the canal and they have steering vehicles with ropes that take the ships through, so they don't crash into the walls. (Don't hold me to it, it is just what I heard they do. Maybe there is a more advanced system now?)

Jesus said this in Matthew: "Enter through the narrow gate. For wide is the gate and broad is the road that leads to destruction, and many enter through it. But small is the gate and narrow the road that leads to life, and only a few find it." (Matthew 7:13-14). As I read the above verses about Jesus, we see that he became flesh. He was in our world. And he had to enter through the small gate and journey on the narrow road. I see this like a ship going through a narrow canal. And the guidelines on either side were managed by vehicles called Grace and Truth. Jesus was full of Grace and full of Truth. These gifts of God guided him in all things on earth. Some on this earth love to talk about grace only. Others only like to focus on the truth. Either way, one cannot navigate a narrow canal with just one guide vehicle. The ship will hit the side. Both are needed for the ship and both are needed in life. As followers of Jesus, we must be full of both grace and truth. And as we dwell with our Savior and experience his grace, we are blessed. Not just once, but over and over again we are blessed. We are blessed with new blessings we could not see before and in new ways we would have never experienced, save by following Jesus. What vast riches are the treasures of God's grace and his truth! Thank you Lord, for all of the ways you truly bless me each and every day. All the honor and glory is yours!

TAKEAWAYS

_____

_____

_____

_____

_____

Day 6

John 1:17-18

For the law was given through Moses; grace and truth came through Jesus Christ. No one has ever seen God, but the one and only Son, who is himself God [God the One and Only] and is in closest relationship with the Father, has made him known.

God's Perfect Reflection

Laws are important in life. They establish the guidelines for acceptable behavior. They also establish the consequences for unacceptable behavior. Without them we would live in evil chaos. I recently visited a resort town in Mexico. As we drove around, the taxi drivers would make jokes about the police officers. About how they were corrupt and greedy. And the advice I got from multiple sources was that if you are driving down there and you are pulled over, don't pay them. Crazy huh? Apparently, sometimes they will pull you over for some false reasons, and then demand a high payment to let you go (a bribe). If you tell them you will not pay they will keep dropping the amount you owe them until finally they will let you go. We decided to take hired vehicles the whole time because of this risk. So we know that laws must exist and are important. In the US, most police are still respected in their communities and enforce the law to the best of their ability. Lately, there have been challenges to law enforcement to try and undermine their position and integrity as a group of public servants. This is a direct attack on the rule of law, I believe. And ultimately what will result is a "cartel-like" system where oppression and fear rule instead of JUSTICE and MERCY.

So what Moses brought was very important to the Jews and it is very important to us today — the law of God. However, what Jesus brought was inexpressibly more important. He was God. As a part of the Trinity, He is at once a distinct personality and God. He was God made flesh to dwell among us and make God known to us. Not just by a book of laws, but by seeing how he acted and cared and called out injustice and spoke truth. He was not defined by what he was for and against any longer. Now, we could SEE WHO HE WAS. Jesus was full of God's Spirit while on earth and he lived a perfect life. This reflection of God —though he gave up some of his heavenly glory, power, and will to become human — was and is such an incredible blessing. What he brought to us in two words was Grace and Truth. If I were to focus on Grace and Truth today, how would this impact my actions? Or my speech? Or my thoughts and judgments? Or my priorities and motives? Would I care so much about "being wronged"? No, I would focus more on speaking truth and administering grace. Lord, help me be a fountain of grace and may my actions and words be an honest reflection of your work in my life. I don't need credit, because I am a sinner saved by grace. So I can be humble and non-judgmental, while still calling out the truth in love and grace. May your Holy Spirit empower me!

TAKEAWAYS

_____

_____

_____

_____

_____

Day 7

John 1:19-23

Now this was John's testimony when the Jewish leaders in Jerusalem sent priests and Levites to ask him who he was. He did not fail to confess, but confessed freely, "I am not the Messiah." They asked him, "Then who are you? Are you Elijah?" He said, "I am not." "Are you the Prophet?" He answered, "No." Finally they said, "Who are you? Give us an answer to take back to those who sent us. What do you say about yourself?" John replied in the words of Isaiah the prophet, "I am the voice of one calling in the wilderness, 'Make straight the way for the Lord.'"

Parallel verses:

I Peter 2:12

Live such good lives among the pagans that, though they accuse you of doing wrong, they may see your good deeds and glorify God on the day he visits us.

Do Others Take Notice?

The Pharisees and teachers of the law were taking notice of John the Baptist. They were interested in how the people flocked to see this poor desert-dweller. So in true fashion of leaders who already have all the answers, they sent some of their disciples to find out about him and his claims to power. John answered their questions with respect, but he also spoke truth. He had lived a good life and served God in his area of calling and mission. His service was practical, preaching and baptizing and shepherding his disciples. And he loved people in God's Spirit.

I love what he says here in answer to his inquirers: "the voice of one calling out in the wilderness, 'Make straight the way for the Lord.'" What does this mean? Since we know he preached repentance from sin, I would choose to interpret this in context. I think this could be another way to say it: "Straighten out your sinful lives and humble your hearts as you prepare for the Lord's arrival. Clean house and be alert to hear the truth and change." John was a man of deep conviction, and he lived this out in life and preached it. Not from a place of arrogance, like he thought he was better than everyone else. He preached it wanting his friends and neighbors to share in the richness of life truly connected to God.

Lord, thank you for sending John the Baptist. He was a model of a humble and repentant, though vocally honest and true, man. May I model my life after him and reflect you and your truth and goodness so much that OTHERS TAKE NOTICE and ask questions.

TAKEAWAYS

_____

_____

_____

_____

_____

Week 1 Top TAKEAWAYS

Look back at the past weeks devotionals and write down your top takeaways.

_____

_____

_____

_____

_____

Action/Implementation Steps

How do you plan to implement these take-aways in your life?

_____

_____

_____

_____

Day 8

John 1:24-31

Now the Pharisees who had been sent questioned him, "Why then do you baptize if you are not the Messiah, nor Elijah, nor the Prophet?" "I baptize with water," John replied, "but among you stands one you do not know. He is the one who comes after me, the straps of whose sandals I am not worthy to untie." This all happened at Bethany on the other side of the Jordan, where John was baptizing. The next day John saw Jesus coming toward him and said, "Look, the Lamb of God, who takes away the sin of the world! This is the one I meant when I said, 'A man who comes after me has surpassed me because he was before me.' I myself did not know him, but the reason I came baptizing with water was that he might be revealed to Israel."

My Cravings ... Do They Lead to Entrapment or Freedom?

Have you ever had cravings for something? I have seen this first hand because my wife had cravings during our pregnancy. She craved some pretty crazy things. But the best craving she had that I remember was the night after our first child was born, she wanted pizza. She was so hungry. Then it became a tradition, and every time she had a baby, we got pizza delivered to the hospital. It was not just any pizza, but Flying Pie Pizza — the best in the valley! (It was my subtle way to incentivize her to have more babies.) It was a small thing to look forward to during a long pregnancy and a challenging delivery. We, as fallen people on

22

this earth, have cravings to sin. In fact our sinful cravings are so strong, they make us slaves to sin. The chains of sin, though invisible, are real and palpable. John came to wake people up and help them be freed from the trappings of sin through repentance. Then, when Jesus came, they would have a clear path to him and not be blinded and deceived by sin. This is why John did not answer the question presented about who he was, but he answered a question of the heart, "Who can free me from these chains of sin?" He pointed to the Savior. He honored and elevated him who was powerful and able to save. Do I honor Jesus today and every day, with my humble heart? Will I redirect questions and/or praise to The One who is deserving of it all?

Lord, teach me to make a clearer path for Jesus in my heart today. May my passion be to pursue and point others to Him. May I crave his goodness instead of sin.

TAKEAWAYS

_____

_____

_____

_____

_____

Day 9

John 1:32-34

Then John gave this testimony: "I saw the Spirit come down from heaven as a dove and remain on him. And I myself did not know him, but the one who sent me to baptize with water told me, 'The man on whom you see the Spirit come down and remain is the one who will baptize with the Holy Spirit.'"

Parallel verses:
Isaiah 61:1-3

The Spirit of the Sovereign Lord is on me, because the Lord has anointed me to proclaim good news to the poor. He has sent me to bind up the brokenhearted, to proclaim freedom for the captives and release from darkness for the prisoners, to proclaim the year of the Lord's favor and the day of vengeance of our God, to comfort all who mourn, and provide for those who grieve in Zion— to bestow on them a crown of beauty instead of ashes, the oil of joy instead of mourning, and a garment of praise instead of a spirit of despair. They will be called oaks of righteousness, a planting of the Lord for the display of his splendor.

<u>Jesus' Anointing by the Spirit of God — What Does It Mean For Me?</u>

When I read this passage in Isaiah, which amplifies John's account of the anointing of God's Spirit on Jesus Christ, it brings such a flood of emotion to my soul — JOY, EXTREME GRATEFULNESS, RELIEF, OVERPOWERING LOVE, and AN IDENTITY IN JESUS CHRIST. This is the spiritual home I come home to every morning — life with Jesus Christ! And why was Jesus anointed, what did the Spirit bring? 1) Am I poor in heart or spirit? He brings me heart-warming good news! I am no longer alone, rejected, cast off by this world. I am now his child. The child of the King! 2) Do I suffer from a broken heart? My mourning will be comforted. The God who created me has provided for this in the person of his Son, Jesus. 3) Am I physically, mentally, emotionally, or spiritually captive to sin or sinful people? Take heart! I have freedom for my soul in Jesus Christ and a relationship with him! 4) Is the darkness around my life palpable? The Light of the World, Jesus Christ, has come to dispel the darkness, to drive it back, and to deliver us from its power. Through his death on the cross, Jesus conquered death and broke its chains! And why did he come to do all this? What will replace this life of captivity to sin and darkness and hopelessness and despair? Jesus came not only to free us but "to bestow on them a crown of beauty instead of ashes, the oil of joy instead of mourning, and a garment of praise instead of a spirit of despair." Praise you Father, Praise you Son, Praise you Spirit, three in one. You have replaced what was dark and evil in my heart with your goodness. I gave you only the ashes left of my life, and you transformed them into beauty! Sin had put me in a perpetual state of mourning, and you brought me a lasting joy! And in place of words of despair, I now speak your words ... I praise your name!

TAKEAWAYS

Day 10

John 1:34-37

I have seen and I testify that this is God's Chosen One. The next day John was there again with two of his disciples. When he saw Jesus passing by, he said, "Look, the Lamb of God!" When the two disciples heard him say this, they followed Jesus.

Parallel verse: [Jesus speaking]
Acts 1:8
But you will receive power when the Holy Spirit comes on you; and you will be my witnesses in Jerusalem, and in all Judea and Samaria, and to the ends of the earth.

All-Out Serving and Getting Out of the Way

I have found in life, many people wander around somewhat aimlessly wondering ... what does God want me to do? What is the point of my life? John searched for and knew his purpose and calling — he was called to prepare the way for the Messiah and to be a witness. This makes me think of someone who prepares the way for a king or queen. Their goal is to make everything as perfect as possible, so the focus and attention can be on the king or queen. If they then step out into the road as the king or queen passes and try to take the attention away from the royalty coming through, they will be cast off or fired. In the same way, many today say they serve God, but they want to take part of the glory as they prepare the way. It is tempting for me too. John the Baptist here is a great model for us. First, he is faithful to minister to the people and call out their sin and baptize them in their repentance. He did this for many years and became quite famous. But once Jesus appeared, he acknowledged that Jesus was the Christ, the Chosen One. And then he simply got out of the way and he pointed to Jesus for others to follow. Two of his disciples left and he welcomed their leaving. Why? Because he understood that his glory would come in eternity, not on earth. And so he served in God's work faithfully, and then he "got out of the way". I hear many today say, "I only want to serve here or in this area of skill". They want to play it safe. But God wants us to risk it all for his kingdom and serve in whatever role or opportunity he opens up to us. I remember that his power is made perfect in weakness! Jesus called his disciples to be his witnesses in Acts, prior to his heavenly ascension. He calls me. Will I be faithful to step out of the way and point to the Savior when he comes or shows his hand in the work around me?

Thank you Lord for your patience with me. You love me in spite of my weaknesses. Fill me to be your witness and help me to lead others to you!

TAKEAWAYS

_____

_____

_____

_____

_____

Day 11
John 1:38-39

Turning around, Jesus saw them following and asked, "What do you want?" They said, "Rabbi" (which means "Teacher"), "where are you staying?" "Come," he replied, "and you will see." So they went and saw where he was staying, and they spent that day with him. It was about four in the afternoon.

The "On" Button of the Gospel

When my wife and I first got married, one of our older family members had just gotten a computer. This person would frequently call my wife and have her help trouble-shoot whatever problems they encountered. Funny thing was, about half the time, after spending 20 or 30 minutes on the phone trying to figure out why it wouldn't work, it came down to pressing the "on" button. Simple. Too simple to think of for this elderly relative. We love this person and they gave us lots of laughs.

John's disciples pulled out a "Jesus tactic" in response to his question — they answered with a question. He asked them, "What do you want?" They answered, "Rabbi, where are you staying?" They communicated a lot in this simple question. First, they called him "Rabbi", this means "teacher". This is what they would have called John the Baptist earlier. They trusted John, so when he said Jesus was greater than he, they sought after Jesus to learn his teachings. Second, they didn't just want to meet him, they wanted to stay with him for a while. They wanted to dwell with him. They wanted to break bread with him and listen to his instruction. "Submit to God and be at peace with him; in this way prosperity will come to you. Accept instruction from his mouth and lay up his words in your heart." (Job 22:21-22) With John the Baptist they have something very good. But they sought Jesus because they wanted something even better! And seeing this faith and the simple obedience they exhibited when John pointed him out as the Messiah, Jesus invited them into his home. What if the Christian life was just that simple? The "on" button is following Jesus. We follow Jesus, call him Rabbi (and Savior and Lord), and ask him where he is staying. By asking this we are asking to join him in his work. It is as if these two disciples said, "John sent us and he told us you are greater than he is. Teacher, show us where you are staying so we can learn your ways and join you in your work!" Jesus likes honesty and boldness in faith. "And without faith it is impossible to please God, because anyone who comes to him must believe that he exists and that he rewards those who earnestly seek him." (Hebrews 11:6) Thank you, Lord, for making it so simple to follow you that even I can't mess it up! You love us and simply desire our loyalty and pledge to follow. Then you open up the "mother lode" — the vast riches of your glory — and bestow upon us gifts we don't deserve. Thank you, Father, for loving even such a sinner as me.

TAKEAWAYS

_____

_____

_____

_____

_____

Day 12

John 1:40-44

Andrew, Simon Peter's brother, was one of the two who heard what John had said and who had followed Jesus. The first thing Andrew did was to find his brother Simon and tell him, "We have found the Messiah" (that is, the Christ). And he brought him to Jesus. Jesus looked at him and said, "You are Simon son of John. You will be called Cephas" (which, when translated, is Peter). The next day Jesus decided to leave for Galilee.

Parallel verses:
Luke 5:4-11

When he had finished speaking, he said to Simon, "Put out into deep water, and let down the nets for a catch." Simon answered, "Master, we've worked hard all night and haven't caught anything. But because you say so, I will let down the nets." When they had done so, they caught such a large number of fish that their nets began to break. So they signaled their partners in the other boat to come and help them, and they came and filled both boats so full that they began to sink. When Simon Peter saw this, he fell at Jesus' knees and said, "Go away from me, Lord; I am a sinful man!" For he and all his companions were astonished at the catch of fish they had taken, and so were James and John, the sons of Zebedee, Simon's partners. Then Jesus said to Simon, "Don't be afraid; from now on you will fish for people." So they pulled their boats up on shore, left everything and followed him.

Demonstrating the Power of God

Peter was called to Jesus in a few ways, and we glean more details about this story from Luke. 1) he was told about him from his brother that he trusted. 2) He heard him preach. (Prior to the above verses in Luke, Jesus had gotten into Peter's boat and asked him to put out a little bit into the water.) 3) He experienced his miraculous ways — he caught a lot of fish. 4) He recognized and repented of his sins.

It is important how we come to Jesus, how we commit to follow him. These are foundational to the faith we build in him. It is the place where it all started. I came to Jesus as a 3-year old. My parents, being new followers of Jesus, were excited to share with us the truth. I accepted him into my heart. A year later, my Mom wanted to make sure I was really serious at 3, and asked me again if I wanted to ask Jesus into my heart. I replied that I didn't need to because I had done that already. Then at 5, God did a miracle in my life. I prayed that it would not hurt, after I broke my arm, when the doctor set it. And God made it so I felt no pain when the doctor set my severely broken arm. We prayed and he answered.

Jesus wanted Peter to know he had the power to provide for and fill him with good things. And he saw ahead to Peter's potential and named him Peter, which means "rock". And as it proved out, he was a rock, a foundational leader, for the church.

What a great model Jesus provides, when calling others to follow. He didn't just try to entice them or beg them to follow. He motivated them by showing them something they didn't have and everyone wanted — the Power of God. And next to this great power — demonstrated by a harvest of tons of fish by just casting on the other side of the boat- the normal way of fishing now seemed kind of pointless.

What is it that Jesus wants to transform in my mind today? How does he intend to change my perspective on what really matters? Will I follow his lead? Lord, you alone are truth and light. You love and lead me into new adventures that involve faith-stretching! I give up. I don't have it all dialed or figured out. You do. Teach me, Lord Jesus!

TAKEAWAYS

_____

_____

_____

_____

_____

Day 13

John 1:45-51

Philip found Nathanael and told him, "We have found the one Moses wrote about in the Law, and about whom the prophets also wrote—Jesus of Nazareth, the son of Joseph." "Nazareth! Can anything good come from there?" Nathanael asked. "Come and see," said Philip. When Jesus saw Nathanael approaching, he said of him, "Here truly is an Israelite in whom there is no deceit." "How do you know me?" Nathanael asked. Jesus answered, "I saw you while you were still under the fig tree before Philip called you." Then Nathanael declared, "Rabbi, you are the Son of God; you are the king of Israel." Jesus said, "You believe because I told you I saw you under the fig tree. You will see greater things than that." He then added, "Very truly I tell you, you will see 'heaven open, and the angels of God ascending and descending on' the Son of Man."

Parallel verses:
Genesis 28:12-15 [speaking of Jacob]
He had a dream in which he saw a stairway resting on the earth, with its top reaching to heaven, and the angels of God were ascending and descending on it. There above it stood the Lord, and he said: "I am the Lord, the God of your father Abraham and the God of Isaac. I will give you and your descendants the land on which you are lying. Your descendants will be like the dust of the earth, and you will spread out to the west and to the east, to the north and to the south. All peoples on earth will be blessed through you and your off-

spring. I am with you and will watch over you wherever you go, and I will bring you back to this land. I will not leave you until I have done what I have promised you."

Nathanael's Faith and His Reward — A Promise

When I was younger, my parents believed they were called to something greater than their ordinary lives. My Dad was a successful and "rising-star" as an electrical engineer and executive in Silicon Valley in the 1970's. He was primed for much of the wealth and greatness this world has to offer. My Mom was serving at our church, one of the singers on Sunday, and managing a household of 6 and sometimes 8 (if my brother and sister from my Dad's first marriage were in town). But God was calling them to something greater. So they sold their house, packed up their belongings and family and went to Bible school. After graduation, my Dad took a position at the San Jose Rescue Mission. It's hard to get more on the front lines than a Rescue Mission. We saw the hungry, the hurting, the refugee, the broken, and the poor from society. My parents were rewarded and their faith grew as they raised support and paid bills on faith. Then, they saw a lot of refugees from Vietnam and Cambodia coming in as they fled from the "Killing Fields". They heard their stories of horror, and my parents knew they needed to know the God of Hope. So they stepped out in faith and started a Bible Study in our home. Little did they know, this Cambodian Bible Study would grow to over 100 Cambodian men, women, and children. Again, their faith was rewarded.

When Nathanael exclaimed, "Rabbi, you are the Son of God", after only just meeting Jesus (and Jesus' telling of seeing him under the fig tree), he exhibited a ton of faith. And Jesus rewarded this faith with a promise and the fulfillment of a well-known prophesy. He would see: 1) heaven open, 2) the angels of God ascending and descending on the Son of Man. This was a well known promise of God to Jacob. In the Genesis passage many, many years earlier, God had promised Jacob: 1) The land he slept on, 2) that his descendants would be as numerous as the sand by the sea, 3) the whole world would be blessed by him and his descendants, and 4) he would watch over him and protect him and he would not leave him. What Jesus was saying to Nathanael was that he would see the angels ascending and descending on him, yes. But, more importantly, he was telling him he was the person who was the fulfillment of this promise in all of its points. Jesus was the fulfillment to Jacob's promise! And Nathanael would experience the fulfillment of the promise God made with Jacob, and see how the world would be blessed through Jesus.

Just like Jacob, my parents stepped out in faith. And they were rewarded. Nine years later, at my Mom's memorial service (she died of cancer), there were over 2,000 people there, and more than half were Cambodian and Vietnamese refugees they had told about Jesus. What a great reward! God ALWAYS REWARDS people who step out in ACTIVE FAITH ... with promises. And HIS PROMISES ARE ALWAYS TRUE. He is trustworthy and deserves my faith today. And I am confident he will reward this faith with his promises!

TAKEAWAYS

_____

_____

_____

_____

_____

Day 14

John 2:1-5

On the third day a wedding took place at Cana in Galilee. Jesus' mother was there, and Jesus and his disciples had also been invited to the wedding. When the wine was gone, Jesus' mother said to him, "They have no more wine." "Woman, why do you involve me?" Jesus replied. "My hour has not yet come." His mother said to the servants, "Do whatever he tells you."

Obey your Parents

Sometimes when we are asked to do something, we may not always realize the reasons why we are asked. I have been asked to do things that feel backwards or unfair, but in the end, they turned out for good. This is in part because I did not see the whole perspective. I have found that many of the things in my life that do not make sense, God uses for his glory in the end. A few examples are my Mom's early death to cancer and most recently the Back the Blue event that I organized. In the first case, God has brought me closer to him over the last 34 years. He allowed my Mom to shine her light brightly to act as a model or example of how to live for God in an "all out" manner. So I must admit, though I wish she was still here every day, I see God's Hand in the aftermath, his loving spirit drawing me and others closer to him, as a result. The Back the Blue event was something God put on my heart. I had helped serve our officers in the past, and this desire to help was in part built on the model my Mom and Dad had given. The event was bigger and more of a commitment than anything else I had done. But

God kept nudging me to serve and obey, so I did, and now a new ministry is continuing to open up.

This passage gives us a glimpse into the heart of Mary, the mother of Jesus. It also gives us a glimpse into the obedience of Jesus her son. Jesus seemingly does not understand why he is being asked to perform this miracle by his Mom. His time "has not yet come." My initial reaction sometimes is the same: "this is not in my comfort zone", "this does not fit into the plans I think God should have for me", or "this will be more effort than I want to give right now, with everything else I have on my plate". But we must notice this — Jesus then obeyed his Mother. He deeply honored her and her friends in this way. And his Mother had faith he would do the right thing. Why did Mary ask him to do this miracle? Couldn't the Feast have gone on with water? I think she understood the culture and the importance of having wine at the wedding to her friend for this special time. Weddings in that time likely took a week to celebrate, and the family needed to provide the food and drink. This would have been a big embarrassment to the family and would have meant all the guests would likely scatter. The wine was a draw. I also think it is interesting that Jesus' first miracle (we will study this tomorrow) was at a wedding on behalf of his mother. God compares his relationship to the church as a bridegroom taking his bride in marriage. The application today is to honor our parents and/or those in authority over us and trust that if they follow God, their "nudges" may be divine. They may have a perspective we do not see.

TAKEAWAYS

_____

_____

_____

Week 2 Top TAKEAWAYS

Look back at the past weeks devotionals and write down your top takeaways.

_____

_____

_____

_____

_____

Action/Implementation Steps

How do you plan to implement these take-aways in your life?

_____

_____

_____

_____

_____

Day 15

John 2:6-11

Nearby stood six stone water jars, the kind used by the Jews for ceremonial washing, each holding from twenty to thirty gallons. Jesus said to the servants, "Fill the jars with water"; so they filled them to the brim. Then he told them, "Now draw some out and take it to the master of the banquet." They did so, and the master of the banquet tasted the water that had been turned into wine. He did not realize where it had come from, though the servants who had drawn the water knew. Then he called the bridegroom aside and said, "Everyone brings out the choice wine first and then the cheaper wine after the guests have had too much to drink; but you have saved the best till now." What Jesus did here in Cana of Galilee was the first of the signs through which he revealed his glory; and his disciples believed in him.

Past the Walls to the Flesh

What do we see in this passage? What do we learn from wine in ceremonial washing basins?

For me, this helps me realize that Jesus cares about the large things... and the seemingly smaller things in our lives. No one was dying or had leprosy or needed food to keep from starving here. But the need was personal; he showed up and gave a great gift to this family and this married couple. It showed he cares about the little things and the things that matter to us. And in doing this, he endeared himself to his mother, his disciples and those around him. He understood that the walls around the hearts of men ...crumble...

when simple acts of compassion break through those walls and meet a heartfelt need.

Jesus broke through in a real way to touch the heartache of poverty, of the broken parents who could not provide all they wanted, or what was expected for their child's wedding. He made their special day more special!

Sometimes, when our hopes are dashed, when we face great embarrassment or a hardship we think difficult to bear, Jesus can change it into a greater blessing! So let us go forth, and look for the simple, seemingly small ways, we can make a difference today — in Jesus' name. He reigns over the large and the small things in our lives and he shows up in the moments. He leads us past the curtain, into the "Holy of Holies" where God resides. And he touch lives deeply — past the walls built up around their hearts — and into the flesh. He is the Great Surgeon and we all need to get some heart-work done. Let us be his instruments to heal others today!

TAKEAWAYS

_____

_____

_____

_____

_____

Day 16

John 2:12-17

After this he went down to Capernaum with his mother and brothers and his disciples. There they stayed for a few days. When it was almost time for the Jewish Passover, Jesus went up to Jerusalem. In the temple courts he found people selling cattle, sheep and doves, and others sitting at tables exchanging money. So he made a whip out of cords, and drove all from the temple courts, both sheep and cattle; he scattered the coins of the money changers and overturned their tables. To those who sold doves he said, "Get these out of here! Stop turning my Father's house into a market!" His disciples remembered that it is written: "Zeal for your house will consume me."

Godly Zeal

Why was Jesus consumed with zeal? Was not the sacrifice of animals required by Jewish law? Yes, it was. But take a look at the first of the Ten Commandments Moses gave. It goes like this: "And the Lord spoke all these words: 'I am the Lord your God, who brought you out of Egypt, out of the land of slavery. You shall have no other God's before me.'" (Exodus 20:1-3) Also consider, in The Sermon on the Mount, Jesus talked about storing up for ourselves treasures in heaven. He discussed that the eyes are the lamp of the whole body. If they are bad, then your whole body will be filled with darkness. He goes on to say this, in Matthew 6:24: "No one can serve two masters. Either he will hate the one and love the other, or he will be devoted to the one and despise the other. You cannot serve both God and Money."

This reminds me of an experience when I was in college. I knew a very poor couple who came to the church where I served as a youth intern. They lived in poverty and were of a very low education. One day, they told me about a business opportunity that was going to help them buy the Clydesdale horses they always dreamed of having. They were going to have a meeting in this opportunity shortly, and invited me to come. I came reluctantly, sensing something was up. As I walked through the door, I'll never forget what I saw: It was as if those greeting me had "$-signs" in their eyes. I knew at once this was a scam and as I listened I was heart-broken. These poor, lowly-educated people were being told if they bought into this multi-level marketing group, all their dreams would come true. It was not true for them or caring, but it was a message full of greed. Why? Because those who shared the message did not care about this couple or their financial health — they cared only about the money they would make off of them. Later in life, when approached by someone else totally unrelated, talking about a business opportunity, I saw the same look in their eyes, the "$-signs" again. I knew it was this same group, before he even told me.

I believe Jesus saw "$-signs" in the eyes of these money-changers. It was all they cared about. They did not care about the hearts of those coming to sacrifice their animals to get right with God. They did not care about honoring God in His temple, or serving him. No level of chaos and disruption at the temple was too much when money was to be made. They served money instead of God. This brings home a good application: what do you and I sacrifice to the god of Money — our time, our relationships with others, or even our relationship with God? This is why Jesus acted in zeal; he saw the hearts of men being deceived. He saw his Father's house being represented as a "Greed-Mongering

Machine"! He simply could not stand for this! It repulsed him at the core of his heart, and it drove him into action.

Zeal is in short supply today. This is different than normal anger, in that it is God-led anger at evil and injustice. Many see things that are "against God" in the church, and they stand by and watch it go on. Shame on us! We need to act like Jesus and call out evil and hypocrisy. We must keep God's church pure. We must also call it out in our hearts, as we are now called a temple of God (see I Peter 2:4-5). Sure your reputation or business may be hurt, but lives are at stake, the light of the gospel is more important! When we see this evil, we must be prepared for it. We must pursue God with such relentless abandon that he will make it clear in the moment, out of our closeness in relationship to him, how to act on His behalf. Zeal is what is required, at times, of a warrior spiritually fully devoted to Christ. If we believe in the truth wholeheartedly, we cannot — no WE WILL NOT — stand by as sin enters God's church. We must act in the full control of His Spirit to reclaim the light of the gospel and redeem it for its truth and power.

TAKEAWAYS

_____

_____

_____

_____

_____

Day 17

John 2:18-22

The Jews then responded to him, "What sign can you show us to prove your authority to do all this?" Jesus answered them, "Destroy this temple, and I will raise it again in three days." They replied, "It has taken forty-six years to build this temple, and you are going to raise it in three days?" But the temple he had spoken of was his body. After he was raised from the dead, his disciples recalled what he had said. Then they believed the scripture and the words that Jesus had spoken.

<u>The Ultimate Rebuild</u>

As I read this passage over, it presents a similar scenario we find quite often today: People wonder on what authority God's children act with such zeal? It is actually a great question and it requires a confident answer. If we do not understand how to answer this question, we risk losing our zeal and our appeal. Jesus answers this in a subtle way, which his disciples pick up on much later in their faith journeys. But when they do ... their faith is greatly strengthened! Let's look at Jesus' answer: "Destroy this temple, and I will raise it again in three days." We must look at this "riddle" in a few ways. 1) What temple is he referring to? 2) What does he mean by rebuilding the temple? 3) What action does he use to accomplish this and what does this action demonstrate to us?

The passage gives us the first answer; he was not referring to the temple building, but to his body, which was a living temple (residing place) of God. (I believe he was also referring to other temples I will detail in #2). This refers to his crucifixion and three days later, his resurrection and ascension into heaven. Second, what did he mean by rebuilding the temple? For this answer, we must consider what changed from the old way of meeting with God in the Temple (a building) and the new way of meeting with God. Prior to Jesus, Jews had to offer sacrifices for the forgiveness of sins and to have a right relationship with God. Now, Jesus FUNDAMENTALLY CHANGED THIS for all time. He paid the price for our sins on the cross. And he ushered in a new way for us to dwell with God. This was symbolized by the tearing in two of the very thick curtain separating the rest of the temple from the Holy of Holies, where the Ark of the Covenant was and where God resided. Before, only the high priest could enter once a year; now we can meet with God individually each day in our hearts. Jesus in his death was the perfect sacrifice, breaking the chains of sin and death (or the hold sin had over all humanity). He then ascended into heaven and he now sits at the right hand of God the Father, as an intercessor for those who believe.

God sees us through the sacrifice of Jesus Christ as pure and clean, if we call on his name. He also sent the Holy Spirit to his believers to live inside us, "God residing in us", which makes us temples of God. So when he said he would rebuild this temple, he meant he would rebuild it in a much better way. It is actually not a physical place anymore — it is a living temple, which is the aggregate of all of the individual temples in all believers' hearts for all time! Now that is a pretty awesome and amazing rebuild! What an upgrade! Finally, we must look at what this action represented. Jesus' action, of coming to earth to be the perfect sacrifice for our sin and rescuing us from a life of sin, to be individually and collectively God's Temple(s), was the ULTIMATE ACT OF SELF-SACRIFICE and the definition of a servant leader.

Philippians 2:5-11 talks about this journey and his servant leadership. "He humbled himself", "he made himself nothing", "and he was obedient unto death— even on a cross"! This is what was attractive to his disciples. This is WHY THEY BELIEVED. They saw a man whose "walk" was stronger that his "talk"! He led by serving. Have you ever struggled with being taken at face value or being believable? WE must lead and gain credibility through serving. We can do the same in our lives — we must submit to God through Jesus Christ and TRULY LIVE! Will we follow the Savior and live as a true Servant-leader today? Life and souls hang in the balance. May we be an accurate reflection of Jesus!

TAKEAWAYS

_____

_____

_____

_____

_____

Day 18

John 2:23-3:2

Now while he was in Jerusalem at the Passover Feast, many people saw the miraculous signs he was doing and believed in his name. But Jesus would not entrust himself to them, for he knew all men. He did not need man's testimony about man, for he knew what was in a man.

Now there was a man of the Pharisees named Nicodemus, a member of the Jewish ruling council. He came to Jesus at night and said, "Rabbi, we know you are a teacher who has come from God. For no one could perform the miraculous signs you are doing if God were not with him.

Serving the Many, Searching For Seekers

We see here one of the keys to Jesus' success in God's eyes on earth: He did not entrust himself to those who praised him. Recognition from the crowd was not needed or desired. How many of us (me included) seek to find recognition from the people around us? And when everything is going great, we can get lost in the moment and think we are amazing and take stock of ourselves. This is a trap. I have had this happen many times. But God is teaching me to let the glory reside in his hands, give him the credit, and look only to him for my worth, my validation, and my recognition. This way, we are not surprised later when some of those who have praised and honored us betray us. Is this being jaded? No. Jesus still loved all in the crowd; he did not turn his back on them. He was being true to his Father and focusing on his will and his ways. And we should do the same. He also was paying attention though, not too caught up in his own glory to miss an opportunity to invest in one close to believing. And we see this reward in chapter 3 — Nicodemus. He came to Jesus under cover of night. He was hungry for the truth, but potentially worried about what others would think of him. He saw Jesus as sent by God and honored him by calling him "Rabbi". Though the Pharisees in general were opposed to Jesus, as he threatened their power and income, Nicodemus was curious. Later we find that he publicly honored Jesus, along with Joseph of Arimathea, after Jesus' death. In John 19:39, Nicodemus brought seventy five pounds of myrrh and aloes to bury Jesus with.

So Nicodemus' curiosity and honesty about Jesus being God overcame his desire for popularity and accolades from those in power. He was transformed from one who was merely curious ... to one who believed. This is our goal as Christ followers. Amidst the crowd, we are to look for those who are curious and seek the truth, and then invest in them. We are not to seek popularity or accolades. If we do we will be disappointed. For man will follow the ways of man in this sinful world. But there will be some who see the light of Jesus Christ and seek after him. We must help them become believers. We must nurture their faith. So today, let us live with a heavenly purpose, not seeking praise from man, but serving God first and foremost! Praise His Almighty Name!

TAKEAWAYS

_____

_____

_____

_____

_____

Day 19

John 3:3-8

Jesus replied, "Very truly I tell you, no one can see the kingdom of God unless they are born again." "How can someone be born when they are old?" Nicodemus asked. "Surely they cannot enter a second time into their mother's womb to be born!" Jesus answered, "Very truly I tell you, no one can enter the kingdom of God unless they are born of water and the Spirit. Flesh gives birth to flesh, but the Spirit gives birth to spirit. You should not be surprised at my saying, 'You must be born again.' The wind blows wherever it pleases. You hear its sound, but you cannot tell where it comes from or where it is going. So it is with everyone born of the Spirit."

The Other-worldly Solution to the Problem of Sin

Reborn. Reconstituted. Regenerated. Renewed. These are terms that are indicative of something old that has been transformed. Jesus understood the fundamental challenge with the heart of man — it is CORRUPT AT THE CORE. Sin has corrupted it. Each of us, by sinning, had/have given over our lives to sin. Sin had/has become our master. If something is corrupted or rotten, it is not easily fixed. It takes significant effort to rid it of its rottenness and rebuild it to where it can thrive. So Jesus tells Nicodemus that in order to see the kingdom of God you must be "born again". Nicodemus responds with a simple question: "How do I re-enter my Mother's womb and be born again?" What I think his question sheds light on is this: he thinks that he was born and may have just stumbled along the way. So if he is reborn in the same way, he can "try harder" next time. Does he think the power to live for God can come out of a corrupted heart? (This is what the Pharisees, the group he belonged to believed). This question is similar to the one people ask today, just in a different way. "I'm a good person, I just make mistakes sometimes", "I do more good than bad", or "I think I deserve another chance to meet God's expectations" — these are all thoughts many have (and many of us have had). But this logic, this reasoning has a FATAL FLAW — it assumes that we, in our own power, can be perfectly good. We cannot! Or it assumes that God will tolerate sin. He does not and will not — he cannot dwell with sin because he is purely good!

So Jesus paints the picture for him. "Flesh gives birth to flesh" means sinful parents will give birth to sinful children. The modeling and raising up of children into adulthood has played this out every time throughout all of time. We live in a world controlled by the Devil and he is strong and powerful. In response, we all have sinned and fallen short of God's glory! But then he introduces the Good News — "the Spirit gives birth to spirit!" If we want a relationship with an "other-worldly" God, we should expect an "out-of-this-world" path to get there. JESUS IS THIS PATH! And as he describes this, he offers us an illustration — The Wind! It is at once exciting, but also high-risk. The wind can bring relief and good things — for sailing and for cooling us down — but it can also be unpredictable and its use involves risk. The problem is, we are unfamiliar with its origins and don't know where it will take us! So we must have faith to use the wind. It is the same with being reborn with God's Spirit. We are charted on a new spiritual course we cannot predict or totally understand. It fundamentally changes us at the core of our hearts. Our life purposes, our mission, our goals and ambitions realign to those of our Father in Heaven. We have the power inside us to truly seek after God in our hearts! We are ... Reborn, Reconstituted, Regenerated, Renewed! Oh, what a risky and wonderful process! Thank you Lord for your Spiritual rebirth in me!

TAKEAWAYS

_____

_____

_____

_____

_____

Day 20

John 3:9-15

"How can this be?" Nicodemus asked. "You are Israel's teacher," said Jesus, "and do you not understand these things? Very truly I tell you, we speak of what we know, and we testify to what we have seen, but still you people do not accept our testimony. I have spoken to you of earthly things and you do not believe; how then will you believe if I speak of heavenly things? No one has ever gone into heaven except the one who came from heaven—the Son of Man. Just as Moses lifted up the snake in the wilderness, so the Son of Man must be lifted up, that everyone who believes may have eternal life in him."

<u>Knowing the One</u>

Jesus sees Nicodemus' desire to understand heavenly things, however he still has a problem understanding or believing the earthly things he preaches. Jesus calls this out, and indicates that until they (the Pharisees) accept Jesus' testimony -- the truth he tells them about God as it pertains to issues on earth -- they will never understand heavenly things. Do we sometimes get ahead of ourselves like Nicodemus and the Pharisees? Do we want to be given the big, glorious responsibilities without being first faithful in the little things? Do we want heavenly recognition without earthly faithfulness? Jesus states it plainly here: he is the only human who has seen heaven, and he is here so that all who believe can have eternal life in heaven too. So following, getting to know, and living like Jesus IS KEY! When we get proud, we tout our accomplishments. When we are humble we realize that we accomplish good things only through the grace of God. This is why Jesus gives the "cutting" remark at the beginning, "You are Israel's teacher and you do not understand these things?" For us to see clearly, the veil of pride must be torn from our eyes. Then and only then can we SEE CLEARLY our sin and our need for a Savior. It seems Nicodemus was in this place. Regardless of our position in life, we must always approach Jesus with the humble heart of a sinner needing a Savior or saved by grace!

TAKEAWAYS

_____

_____

_____

_____

_____

Day 21

John 3:16-18 AMP

"For God so [greatly] loved and dearly prized the world, that He [even] gave His [One and] only begotten Son, so that whoever believes and trusts in Him [as Savior] shall not perish, but have eternal life. For God did not send the Son into the world to judge and condemn the world [that is, to initiate the final judgment of the world], but that the world might be saved through Him. Whoever believes and has decided to trust in Him [as personal Savior and Lord] is not judged [for this one, there is no judgment, no rejection, no condemnation]; but the one who does not believe [and has decided to reject Him as personal Savior and Lord] is judged already [that one has been convicted and sentenced], because he has not believed and trusted in the name of the [One and] only begotten Son of God [the One who is truly unique, the only One of His kind, the One who alone can save him]."

The Great Gift

Do you realize that you are GREATLY LOVED and DEEPLY PRIZED by the God of the universe? WOW! A little recap ... Jesus cleared the merchants from the temple and performed miracles — and the Jewish leaders challenged him, but the crowd loved him for it. So in comes Nicodemus, a representative of the Pharisees, who sneaks out to meet with Jesus. We don't know for sure his motivation, but Jesus sees an opportunity. He first tells him he must be born again, born of God's Spirit. And then he chastised him for being Israel's teacher but not understanding the simple earthly things he spoke of. How could he understand heavenly things and their implications on earth? Now, the SPIRITUAL BOMBSHELL — Jesus opens up God's MASSIVE HEART for mankind to Nicodemus. He tells him God's Love is so great for him that God gave The One and Only, his only Son, The Promised Messiah. The result is eternal life for all who actively believe in His name. This is an incredible gift and it was likely not fully understood at the time. Maybe today many don't understand this gift. Some may not want to put in the time to fully fathom it. To others, it convicts them of sin, and they shy away (why would they need God's gift, unless they were guilty of sin)? And it comes with a heavy promise of final judgment: those who actively believe and follow Jesus will have eternal life. Those who reject this gift ... they are condemned in their sin. Some might think this is unkind, to condemn people. But it is clear that judgment was pending for sins before Jesus came. Some will choose to forgo salvation, and keep their pride. To continue to act like they have it all together, to dress up the outside while the inside is corrupted with sin. This is not God's fault, but their personal decision to continue to reject him, despite such a huge personal sacrifice. Jesus Christ is God's One and Only Begotten Son. And he came to earth to die for me; and for you; and for our neighbors; and for our family; and for those who are dirty, hard to love, prideful, and greedy. He came to love all, and those who seek after him will receive this great gift of love. Drink deeply of its vastness and truth, my friends! It never fails to overwhelm and surprise us in its GREAT GOODNESS! Praise God and his Son, Jesus, for their amazing sacrifice!

TAKEAWAYS

Week 3 Top TAKEAWAYS

Look back at the past weeks devotionals and write down your top takeaways.

_____

_____

_____

_____

_____

Action/Implementation Steps

How do you plan to implement these take-aways in your life?

_____

_____

_____

_____

_____

Day 22

John 3:19-21

"This is the verdict: Light has come into the world, but men loved darkness instead of light because their deeds were evil. Everyone who does evil hates the light, and will not come into the light for fear that his deeds will be exposed. But whoever lives by the truth comes into the light, so that it may be seen plainly that what he had done has been done through God." [Jesus speaking]

Multi-faceted Reflectors

When did life become so black and white? When did we start to see such anger towards God and his church? What we are experiencing now in America is likely the beginning of what other Christians have experienced all over the world for years and years — True Persecution for one's faith. Many wonder why this persecution is done. It is because the truth exposes sin. The Bible mentions other contracts too, like good vs. evil and life vs. death. Jesus caps off his conversation with Nicodemus by comparing true followers to those who are not. Just like there are true believers and non-believers — there are those who STEP OUT INTO THE LIGHT to give glory to God and those who stay in the darkness.

Evil can show itself overtly or covertly in our lives. Some do evil acts in the open. Others are complicit and watch these acts being done without raising a finger to stop them. In contrast, you have true believers who stand for what is right and good in life. They are not perfect, but they are committed to seeking after righteousness. II Corinthians 4:6-7 says,

"For God, who said, 'Let light shine out of darkness,' made his light shine in our hearts to give us the light of the knowledge of the glory of God in the face of Christ. But we have this treasure in jars of clay to show that this all-surpassing Power is from God and not from us." What a great gift we have been given, "the light of the knowledge of the glory of God in the face of Christ." When we step out in the light, it is clearly seen that we are broken, ordinary vessels — jars of clay. This is just fine, because it allows the truth to be seen for what it is. God's light SHINES through us, accomplishing his work in and through our committed hearts. I have used the analogy of myself as a man full of scars and holes. I have fallen and been picked up by a forgiving Savior time and again. When I serve, I try to be transparent, because then people can see that if God can use a broken man like me, he can use them too. Some try to cover up their weaknesses/sin/holes in life. This attempt to look good on the outside is never very attractive and it keeps the light from shining through. Light shines through holes brightly. Scars are areas where I have had to be healed, sometimes from things done to me, other times by sins I committed. When God forgives us he heals us, but scars are left. Some think these are not becoming, and by themselves they are not. However, God's Light reflects off these scars in a fascinating diversion of light, like off of a multi-faceted diamond. This reflection catches the eyes of others. It is incredibly beautiful to see God's light reflecting off of our healed scars. So the truth is, the more we let God shine through us and reflect off of us, HE IS GLORIFIED! When we cover up our sin and we turn from him and his light — the Light of the World — we become dim. Our confidence comes from him. So let's shine his light brightly today. May we be multi-faceted reflectors of His Glory.

TAKEAWAYS

_____

_____

_____

_____

_____

Day 23

John 3:22-30

After this, Jesus and his disciples went out into the Judean countryside, where he spent some time with them, and baptized. Now John also was baptizing at Aenon near Salim, because there was plenty of water, and people were coming and being baptized. (This was before John was put in prison.) An argument developed between some of John's disciples and a certain Jew over the matter of ceremonial washing. They came to John and said to him, "Rabbi, that man who was with you on the other side of the Jordan—the one you testified about—look, he is baptizing, and everyone is going to him." To this John replied, "A person can receive only what is given them from heaven. You yourselves can testify that I said, 'I am not the Messiah but am sent ahead of him.' The bride belongs to the bridegroom. The friend who attends the bridegroom waits and listens for him, and is full of joy when he hears the bridegroom's voice. That joy is mine, and it is now complete. He must become greater; I must become less."

Backseat Joy

Suppose an expert harbor pilot, one who takes ships through the sometimes dangerous waters of the harbor, was also asked to unload the cargo as well, using a crane. The problem is, he had not been given this skill or training. This might result in unexpected delays and potentially dangerous situations. John the Baptist here knew his role in God's team. He was the one who came before Jesus to prepare the way. His baptism was before Jesus came, and it was for repentance of sin. Jesus baptized believers in his Name. When we TAKE JOY in what abilities God has given us and the mission he set us on, we are focused on our blessings. When we compare, as John's disciples were doing, (likely envious of Jesus' successes) then we lose sight of who we are serving and whose opinion matters. Matthew 23:10-12 says this: "Nor are you to be called instructors, for you have one Instructor, the Messiah. The greatest among you will be your servant. For those who exalt themselves will be humbled, and those who humble themselves will be exalted." Doesn't this seem backwards in comparison to how the world operates? John the Baptist is a good model of Servant Leadership. He took what he was given from God and lived it. He did not worry about others who were getting more recognition. He focused on pleasing his master. He also was joyful at other people's successes. He was overjoyed to see Jesus emerge and was happy to take a back seat. Can I be happy at the successes of others and enable them? Will I see the big picture of God's work and take joy in my role? How will I respond when I am called to let the focus be on someone else?

TAKEAWAYS

Day 24
John 3:31-34

The one who comes from above is above all; the one who is from the earth belongs to the earth, and speaks as one from the earth. The one who comes from heaven is above all. He testifies to what he has seen and heard, but no one accepts his testimony. Whoever has accepted it has certified that God is truthful. For the one whom God has sent speaks the words of God, for God gives the Spirit without limit.

The Spirit — A Gift Without Limit

How do I speak — as one from this earth? Or do I speak as a citizen of a heavenly kingdom? My spiritual hometown matters! Jesus was the one sent from Heaven to earth, and when we follow him we learn to speak as he spoke on earth. Jesus was above all. This means he was granted authority over all by his birthright. And so he does not need to theorize or pontificate about God, who he is, what matters to him, and how he works. HE KNOWS HIS HEART. He has consulted with him in his throne room. He saw his hand in action! And when we believe in Jesus Christ as our Lord and Savior, we certify that God is truthful, because God declared at Jesus' baptism that Jesus was his Son. And the one God sent speaks his words. How do I know this? Because God gives His Spirit without limit. This has been proven throughout Jewish history; just look at the lives of Moses, Elijah, Daniel, and David. And Jesus was full of God's Spirit, as well.

Do I feel full of God's Spirit? Do I truly believe God will fill me full of His Spirit? When we accept Jesus into our heart as Lord and Savior, we gain the Holy Spirit in our hearts. And when God gives the Spirit, he gives the Spirit WITH-OUT LIMIT! Oh, what limitless power and love I can have with the gift of "The Spirit without limit". Incredible! Lord, I believe today that you give me your Spirit without limit. May your Spirit enable me to shine your grace and love and truth to all those around me today.

TAKEAWAYS

_____

_____

_____

_____

_____

Day 25

John 3:35-36

The Father loves the Son and has placed everything in his hands. Whoever believes in the Son has eternal life, but whoever rejects the Son will not see life, for God's wrath remains on them.

Parallel verses:

Colossians 1:15-20

The Son is the image of the invisible God, the firstborn over all creation. For in him all things were created: things in heaven and on earth, visible and invisible, whether thrones or powers or rulers or authorities; all things have been created through him and for him. He is before all things, and in him all things hold together. And he is the head of the body, the church; he is the beginning and the firstborn from among the dead, so that in everything he might have the supremacy. For God was pleased to have all his fullness dwell in him, and through him to reconcile to himself all things, whether things on earth or things in heaven, by making peace through his blood, shed on the cross.

Power Over All Things

Many professional athletes hire sports agents and these agents negotiate the terms of multi-million dollar contracts for them. In fact, some of these contracts are now reaching up to a 1/3 of a billion dollars over 10 years or so. The best agent, it seems, gets the best players. And he holds the cards for them and plays them expertly to maximize the value for the player ($'s, preferred location, opportunity to play in the post-season, etc.). It can seem that he holds all things relative to this player and their career in his hands for a little while. In reality, there are so many variables, no one earthly person can really hold much in their hands. The devil, when he tempted Jesus in the desert, bragged about having control of all things, but it was a part-truth and only true for a season. The truth is, God holds all things in his hands; he always has and he always will. And he granted control over all things to his Son, Jesus Christ. All things includes my family, my job, my reputation, my city, state, country, and world. Our whole universe. All things big and all things small! So in life, do I want to experience a taste of supernatural? Do I want to see God's glory on this earth? I can if I submit to his Son, Jesus Christ. All of the fullness of God dwells in Jesus. He is the image of the invisible God. And the crazy, incredible thing is ... he can work through me to accomplish all things! Thank you, Lord Jesus, for valuing a sinner like me and elevating me to a brother and front man for your kingdom. You reign in all that is life. I commit to letting you reign in my life too. Use me to accomplish your will today!

TAKEAWAYS

Day 26
John 4:1-6

Now Jesus learned that the Pharisees had heard that he was gaining and baptizing more disciples than John— although in fact it was not Jesus who baptized, but his disciples. So he left Judea and went back once more to Galilee. Now he had to go through Samaria. So he came to a town in Samaria called Sychar, near the plot of ground Jacob had given to his son Joseph. Jacob's well was there, and Jesus, tired as he was from the journey, sat down by the well. It was about noon.

Taking the Direct Route to Restore

Routes in life matter. I am reminded of a trip I took with my family to go from Meridian, ID to Bozeman, MT to attend a family wedding. My kids still tease me about this trip to this day. We were in Northern Idaho heading up to Bozeman, and I had to take a client call. After I got back in the car and turned the map on, I followed it. A while later we started to go into a subdivision. I came to rest at a residential house. Problem was, I was supposed to be at a park in Bozeman. Instead I was in Helena, MT. Somehow my cell phone map app reprogrammed after my call and I was guided to the wrong address. It took us 90 minutes to get back and we were late for the rehearsal dinner.

In contrast, Jesus was taking the short route (not as directionally challenged as I am), but most of the Jews preferred the longer route. Why? Because by taking the longer route, they would not have to associate with the "half-breed" Samaritans (as they referred to them). They were a race of Jews that inter-married with the surrounding people-groups. The Samaritans worshipped God and mixed in some pagan practices and did not keep all of the strict rules of the Jews.

Jesus went the short way, but this was the way most would not go. True, he was likely saving a day and a half of walking. But there is something deeper here. It was hypocritical for the Jews to say they followed God and then to not love their neighbors, the Samaritans. Jesus was going to those who were outcasts to care for them. He was not going to skirt around an uncomfortable situation. And as we will find out in the next devotional, he addressed it with love and grace.

Where do my routes in life take me? Will I allow myself to be taken into uncomfortable situations to serve the Lord? In life, do I just play it safe? Will I allow God to stretch my faith?

Thank you, Lord, for the courage to be direct, take the direct routes in life, and call out hypocrisy in the church. May I act as you did, going to those who are hurting and broken and showing them the source of true spiritual life.

TAKEAWAYS

_____

_____

_____

_____

_____

Day 27
John 4:7-10

When a Samaritan woman came to draw water, Jesus said to her, "Will you give me a drink?" (His disciples had gone into the town to buy food.) The Samaritan woman said to him, "You are a Jew and I am a Samaritan woman. How can you ask me for a drink?" (For Jews do not associate with Samaritans.) Jesus answered her, "If you knew the gift of God and who it is that asks you for a drink, you would have asked him and he would have given you living water."

Parallel verses:
Matthew 5:16

In the same way, let your light shine before others, that they may see your good deeds and glorify your Father in heaven.

A Shocking Love

When I was in Junior College, I did not have a financial backer to help me get through. I had served as a youth intern at a church and was trying to finish out my second year. But I was in a tough financial position and I wasn't sure how I was going to pay for my final year of junior college. I called my Dad. I told him the situation. My Dad was in the ministry, and I don't think he had a lot of money. But he called and told me that one of his supporters was going to send me a check for $5,000 as a loan. I was blown away. It was exactly what I needed. After I graduated from my 4-year school, Pacific Lutheran University, I was set to start making payments. I made the first two, and then this nice couple told me they forgave my loan. They didn't even know me! I was blown away. What a great gift.

Jesus had given this woman at the well a great gift. She had lived under the impression that Jews thought of her as a "second-rate" citizen, not to be associated with. She, was hurting and Jesus validated her by speaking to her and asking her for help. HE ELEVATED HER above himself. All of the things that had pushed her down the societal scale: being a Samaritan, being a woman, and (as we will find out elsewhere in her story) being married multiple times, were, in one moment of love and care, erased. She almost couldn't believe it was true. This is why she said: "How can you ask me for a drink?"

She was shocked and bewildered that Jesus, a Jewish Rabbi, would humble himself to show a place of need and ask her for help. That he would validate her, though she was a Samaritan and a woman ... and THAT SHE IN FACT MATTERED! He treated her like a person first and not a member of a group.

And in this way he let his light shine before men! This is the light of God in action and it is EXTREMELY ATTRACTIVE! When we seek out the needy and the hurting and value them, we shine God's light into their hearts.

How can I live without boundaries today? How can I show those who are outcasts around me that they matter to me and to Jesus too? How can I WOW them with kindness and humble myself in their presence?

Lord, thank you for modeling a piercing and surprising love for the outcast. Teach me Lord, teach me to elevate others and humble myself.

TAKEAWAYS

_____

_____

_____

_____

_____

Day 28

John 4:10-14

Jesus answered her, "If you knew the gift of God and who it is that asks you for a drink, you would have asked him and he would have given you living water." "Sir," the woman said, "you have nothing to draw with and the well is deep. Where can you get this living water? Are you greater than our father Jacob, who gave us the well and drank from it himself, as did also his sons and his livestock?" Jesus answered, "Everyone who drinks this water will be thirsty again, but whoever drinks the water I give them will never thirst. Indeed, the water I give them will become in them a spring of water welling up to eternal life."

Radiating Hope

Hope is a powerful thing. It can be expanded or at times seem to be taken away. There are times in my life when hope seemed all but lost: when my Mom died, when a business failed, or when I have acted in sin and hurt those around me. There are other times when hope was restored and resurrected in my life; when I was given new life in situations by God or others. These times were transformative to how I operated going forward. I no longer needed the same coping mechanisms to deal with the stress, loneliness, or challenges in life. Instead, I had NEW HOPE! Some examples of these times of new hope are: 1) Seeing God provide me with a wife from afar, when I was clueless on how to date women and 2) Seeing him provide a job for my wife at a 30% increase in pay from the job she left 4 years prior, when my business had failed.

What fascinates me about this story of the Samaritan woman is the hope for something greater that Jesus presents. Jesus was physically thirsty, but this woman was thirsty in life. They found some common ground. The thrills of the sinful life had not satisfied her (they never do). So Jesus is telling her that she can drink water that will not only quench her thirst, but internally fill her up with hope! Hope for eternal life. And he would then show her the way to this eternal life. He radiated the Hope in his heart to her.

How am I going to share hope today with others ... the hope for eternal life? Am I full of the hope of God myself? Do I speak as one who has a great hope in life? Do I act that way?

Lord, help me to speak and act from a place of peace and assurance in my hope in Jesus Christ. May I RADIATE this HOPE into the lives of others today!

TAKEAWAYS

Week 4 Top TAKEAWAYS

Look back at the past weeks devotionals and write down your top takeaways.

_____

_____

_____

_____

_____

Action/Implementation Steps

How do you plan to implement these takeaways in your life?

_____

_____

_____

_____

_____

Day 29

John 4:15-19

The woman said to him, "Sir, give me this water so that I won't get thirsty and have to keep coming here to draw water." He told her, "Go, call your husband and come back." "I have no husband," she replied. Jesus said to her, "You are right when you say you have no husband. The fact is, you have had five husbands, and the man you now have is not your husband. What you have just said is quite true." "Sir," the woman said, "I can see that you are a prophet."

Receive And Believe — God Wants To Work The Impossible In Me! (and my birthday wish)

I imagine between the call-out on her relational sin and her recognizing he was a prophet, there might have been a tear or two shed. But she saw something of God in Jesus and investigated. There are times in my life when I have seen the things of God and I almost wrote them off. One comes to mind. A few years back, God put on my heart to plan and hold a Back the Blue Rally. And I had never done anything close to this before. I loved supporting the police, but we were in the middle of COVID. I wrestled with God in prayer for a week. He won! We planned and held a rally at the largest center in Idaho, raised $43,000 in sponsorships, and had over 1,000 people there during COVID, on a Monday night. We had speakers, including a former law enforcement officer fly in from New York (who was at 9/11 in New York and is a Fox News contributor), we had a local Sheriff, and Police Chief, the Governor and Lt. Governor of Idaho, and our MC was the most recognizable name in law enforcement training, Paul Butler from South Carolina. We had a concert, as well. And we did all of this in just 6 weeks. Event planners (who do this for a living) told me this was impossible for them to imagine doing this in just six weeks. It normally takes a whole year to plan. All of this ... God brought to the doorstep of a corporate insurance salesman in Idaho, simply because I believed him with the impossible.

Two and a half years later, a new, non-political ministry to police officers is budding, with 20 volunteers and we have held 2 rallies. More importantly, we are making personal connections with these officers and encouraging them, and helping promote the good things they do every day. These devotionals are starting to work their way into Police circles. We are currently in the process of cutting an inspirational video to encourage them on the job and to train them how to deal with being shot and overcome adversity by pivoting to something good. This is based on a story of experiences by Sergeant Brad Childers of the Nampa Police Department. We also are sending some awesome, handmade wood "blue-line" flags to an officer (and his family) who was almost killed, one for the family and one for a benefit fundraiser. The flags are donated by a kind man named Brad, who is called to make them and very gifted. These are going to be signed by the officer's department. I get to participate in this wonderful ministry simply because I BELIEVED GOD for the impossible when he called me to serve. And to think. I almost dismissed the call and missed the blessing, because I didn't think it was possible.

This is an interesting passage, as we see some different things at play here: coping mechanisms, unbelief in the seemingly impossible, and finally the realization of truth. First, the woman at the well (Joe's interpretation) jokes with Jesus about this living water. I imagine a wry smile and hands thrown up in the air, while she says, "Give me this water so I don't have to come down here to draw water again." She probably thought he was teasing her. It was too far of a stretch for her to believe. And when she was being teased and made fun of in the past, she likely resorted to joking. She couldn't see the spiritual application and spiritual significance of Jesus' LIVING WATER welling up in her! She didn't think she was worthy. How many times do I dismiss the spiritual because it does not seem practical in my physical world? Or I don't think I am worthy or skilled enough to participate? And so Jesus graciously showed her his authority over this world. He asks her to get her husband. OUCH! But Jesus shows her HE KNOWS HER PAIN. Instead of pushing her away and putting her down for her sin, what does he do with this? He showed her TRUE LOVE AND COMPASSION. How can I show others in my life, in a kind way, I understand their pain and care about them? And then, in one statement, he helped her cross over from the physical into the spiritual; cross over from seeing life for its hardships to seeing life for its spiritual possibilities! AND SHE BELIEVED! She left behind years of mistakes and pain and took a step forward to believe in God's Son.

We have a plaque hanging on our wall year round that reads: Good Things Come To Those Who Believe!

Today is my 49th birthday, and my Birthday Wish is this: that each of us will choose today to BELIEVE GOD FOR THE IMPOSSIBLE -- for something really good and really difficult.

Thank you Lord for caring so much about the Samaritan woman at the well and also caring so much about me. You gave her many opportunities to see past her human limitations and into YOUR LIMITLESS POWER & GRACE. And you have done this so many times for me! Help me to continue to believe that WITH YOU, ANYTHING is possible!

TAKEAWAYS

_____

_____

_____

_____

_____

Day 30

John 4:19-26

"Sir," the woman said, "I can see that you are a prophet. Our ancestors worshiped on this mountain, but you Jews claim that the place where we must worship is in Jerusalem." "Woman," Jesus replied, "believe me, a time is coming when you will worship the Father neither on this mountain nor in Jerusalem. You Samaritans worship what you do not know; we worship what we do know, for salvation is from the Jews. Yet a time is coming and has now come when the true worshipers will worship the Father in the Spirit and in truth, for they are the kind of worshipers the Father seeks. God is spirit, and his worshipers must worship in the Spirit and in truth." The woman said, "I know that Messiah (called Christ) is coming. When he comes, he will explain everything to us." Then Jesus declared, "I, the one speaking to you—I am he."

True Worshippers

Worship is an interesting word. It is more than just songs and hymns sung in a church or a temple. Worship means devoting yourself to someone or something, that all of your energy and heart is focused on what pleases this person or thing. The problem with worship in Jesus' time, as in ours, is it mostly focused on the created things instead of the Creator. The Jews, much before Jesus' time, had issues with shifting their worship to idols. A perfect example was the Golden Calf. They also worshipped the evil gods of those people groups around them, like Baal and others. In Jesus' time, many Jews worshipped their man-made systems of rules and protocols, in their attempts to look righteous on the outside. This is evidenced by their self-righteousness and rejection of the Samaritans, by race. Jesus came to this woman, and later to these people, and introduced TRUE WORSHIP — that which is BY SPIRIT AND IN TRUTH. It starts with a heart that has opened up to Jesus. He comes in and works on our hearts, no matter how messed up we are or what poor shape we are in because of sin. We hear this woman's belief in the Messiah. She believes his message will be different from the one of hatred and prejudice that she had experienced from the Jews. She had already been searching and waiting for the Messiah. And then ... Jesus gives her a gift and tells her he is the Messiah!

The honest truth is we all need a Savior, and each of our hearts are broken beyond repair, save for his healing touch. When we repent of our sins and ask Jesus to be our Lord and our Savior, we give him the right to steer the course of our lives. In return, he allows our spirit to dwell with the Holy Spirit, the third part of the triune Godhead. This is what Jesus meant when he said true worshippers will worship in spirit. This relationship with God then allows for us to have the confidence to be truly honest about life — our victories and our shortcomings. When we rely on God in our weaknesses, we are strong! Let us resist the temptation to practice church and throw life into autopilot mode. Instead, we can truly worship the Lord if we are humble and believe!

TAKEAWAYS

_____

_____

_____

_____

Day 31

John 4:27-39

Just then his disciples returned and were surprised to find him talking with a woman. But no one asked, "What do you want?" or "Why are you talking with her?" Then, leaving her water jar, the woman went back to the town and said to the people, "Come, see a man who told me everything I ever did. Could this be the Messiah?" They came out of the town and made their way toward him. Meanwhile his disciples urged him, "Rabbi, eat something." But he said to them, "I have food to eat that you know nothing about." Then his disciples said to each other, "Could someone have brought him food?" "My food," said Jesus, "is to do the will of him who sent me and to finish his work. Don't you have a saying, 'It's still four months until harvest'? I tell you, open your eyes and look at the fields! They are ripe for harvest. Even now the one who reaps draws a wage and harvests a crop for eternal life, so that the sower and the reaper may be glad together. Thus the saying 'One sows and another reaps' is true. I sent you to reap what you have not worked for. Others have done the hard work, and you have reaped the benefits of their labor." Many of the Samaritans from that town believed in him because of the woman's testimony.

Eyes Open Wide to the Harvest

2016 was an amazing presidential election year. Donald Trump, a non-polished politician, took the Republican Party by storm, held large rallies and beat Hillary Clinton for the presidency. He was not everyone's first choice, and there were many who predicted his failure, but he proved them all wrong. Once in office, outside of the poor surface level communications skills, he accomplished a lot of things people thought were not possible: an historic economic recovery, bringing manufacturing jobs back to the US, a Middle East peace accord, tariffs on China which forced them to back down and work on a new trade deal, withdrawing our troops from wars in other countries across the world, forcing other countries to pay their share in NATO, calling the North Korean president's bluff, etc. Whether you like him (or his tactics) or you don't he did accomplish quite a bit in his four years.

In the early days, the reactions of people to Trump were either fully onboard or against him. Not comparing Trump to Jesus at all, but the reactions to Jesus reminded me of many people's reaction to Trump in some odd ways. Jesus was also a polarizing figure (though in not the same ways).

Some people got what Jesus was doing and embraced him wholeheartedly; others just hated the man and could not accept his ministry. Some were late followers like doubting Thomas, and many were confused as to his purpose. Take a look at how the Samaritan woman responds: she left her jar and went into town and spread the news about Jesus to all around. It sounds like she was a believer. Then the disciples came back and were at first surprised that he was talking to a Samaritan woman in public, then focused on his food intake. They MISSED THE WHOLE REASON why the woman left her jar at the well. We find also that many believed because of this woman's testimony and some did not. Later on, more believed as Jesus spoke.

It is similar in life. The reactions to revolutionary truths vary in people. There are the 1) early adaptors, 2) the lagging believers, 3) those who never seem to quite understand, 4) and those who refuse to believe, though the evidence is so close to them it could hit them upside the head. Jesus calls this out in addressing his disciples regarding his "food" with an analogy: he gets fed as he does God's spiritual work in the hearts of people. This is much more exciting and fulfilling than even eating food when super hungry. Then he says to them, "OPEN YOUR EYES and look at the fields!" It is almost as if he is saying, "Hello guys, can you not see what just happened and is happening now? God's message of the gospel of salvation is being spread! We found a true believer! She is out harvesting souls for eternal life. You should join her!"

This is what I feel like is happening today. People are worried more about jobs, food, viruses, fairness, and national racial tensions than the gospel of Jesus Christ. Friends, join me in opening your eyes and looking at the fields. They are ripe for the harvest of souls unto eternal life! So let's get busy!

TAKEAWAYS

_____

_____

_____

_____

_____

Day 32

John 4:39-42

Many of the Samaritans from that town believed in him because of the woman's testimony, "He told me everything I ever did." So when the Samaritans came to him, they urged him to stay with them, and he stayed two days. And because of his words many more became believers. They said to the woman, "We no longer believe just because of what you said; now we have heard for ourselves, and we know that this man really is the Savior of the world."

<u>Refreshing Fountains of Life</u>

Today we see The Harvest — the collecting of the rewards from a lot of hard work. From all the way back to Abraham, God cared about these people and he had Abraham build a well here. This well created a center for people to live around, as water is a necessity of life. It sustains growth and hydrates people and animals and plants. So too, Jesus is the source of life. He is the SPRING OF OVERFLOWING WATER inside our souls.

I find it interesting that the people's ears were opened to hearing by the woman's testimony, and then they listened to Jesus and became committed followers on their own. They owned their faith! And so we have presented here, in the story of the Samaritan Woman, a great formula or model of how to witness relationally: 1) Find some common ground and show God's love, 2) Make an analogy between that common ground and life in touch with God Spirit, 3) Blow their minds with the truth of the gospel, 4) Challenge them to leave their ways of sin, 5) and

Teach and mentor those who follow in the Word of God. Jesus saw the spiritual opportunity with a heart that was ready for something more in life, and he connected and loved this woman from the heart. The result was a great harvest of souls for eternity. Today, we are in a world where many people are looking for meaning in life and they are searching for truth — something more. Changing life's way of operating (COVID, job losses, polarizing elections) creates a fertile environment for growing faith and ultimately harvesting souls. This season of uncertainty in life reminds me of the plowing phase in farming. Everything gets stirred up, mixed up, as what was on the bottom is now on the top. God is calling us to be fountains of refreshing water to a lost world. Lord, help me to live well and look for those opportunities to challenge people towards truth and help them get there with you. Help me not to get too caught up in the things of this world and miss the Harvest!

TAKEAWAYS

_____

_____

_____

_____

_____

Day 33

John 4:43-54

After the two days he left for Galilee. (Now Jesus himself had pointed out that a prophet has no honor in his own country.) When he arrived in Galilee, the Galileans welcomed him. They had seen all that he had done in Jerusalem at the Passover Festival, for they also had been there. Once more he visited Cana in Galilee, where he had turned the water into wine. And there was a certain royal official whose son lay sick at Capernaum. When this man heard that Jesus had arrived in Galilee from Judea, he went to him and begged him to come and heal his son, who was close to death. "Unless you people see signs and wonders," Jesus told him, "you will never believe." The royal official said, "Sir, come down before my child dies." "Go," Jesus replied, "your son will live." The man took Jesus at his word and departed. While he was still on the way, his servants met him with the news that his boy was living. When he inquired as to the time when his son got better, they said to him, "Yesterday, at one in the afternoon, the fever left him." Then the father realized that this was the exact time at which Jesus had said to him, "Your son will live." So he and his whole household believed. This was the second sign Jesus performed after coming from Judea to Galilee.

The Persistent Official of Faith Who Petitioned Jesus

First, I find it interesting here that there is a note that while he was welcomed in Galilee, he was not shown the honor due a prophet. Jesus was from Nazareth of Galilee and this was about 8-10 miles south of Cana. And Samaria was farther south still. So coming from Samaria, he would have gone through his hometown and then onto Cana. Reality was, he loved those he grew up around, but their faith was small and they likely still saw him as the little kid they once knew. They could not see that God had given him the ministry of a prophet and he served the people in love and truth like a prophet of God. Do I see people as God sees them, especially those close to me ... my family and friends? Or do I dismiss them because I remember when they were in diapers and were a dependent child?

Second, here in Cana we see he is respected by an outsider, a public official from a distant town. This official from Capernaum comes to him and asks him to heal his son who is dying. He traveled about 20 miles to see Jesus. He begged Jesus to come and heal his son. Jesus commented that the people had little faith, and unless they saw miraculous signs they would not believe. Then he healed the son remotely with a word. Upon traveling back and confirming this was true, the man and his whole family were saved. Here are some takeaways from this passage: 1) Jesus loves persistent petitions. He likes to see a sold-out heart. This official would not take no for an answer. And Jesus rewarded him for this persistence by doing a miraculous healing. Will I pray for those I love persistently? 2) We, as people, are typically of the "low-faith" variety. We like to see things before we believe in them. Jesus was looking for someone like this official who took the Son of God at his word and believed him. Jesus can heal my heart and fix my challenges by a simple word. Do I believe it? 3) Finally, this man's faith in Jesus led his whole family to follow the Messiah, God's Chosen One. He testified of the truth to them. How does my faith shine into the hearts of those around me, my family and friends? Will it compel them to trust God with their lives too?

Lord, thank you for realizing that I have a weak faith and it needs to be built up. May I trust you to do your good, faith-building work in me! Thank you, Father!

TAKEAWAYS

_____

_____

_____

_____

_____

Day 34
John 5:1-15

Some time later, Jesus went up to Jerusalem for one of the Jewish festivals. Now there is in Jerusalem near the Sheep Gate a pool, which in Aramaic is called Bethesda and which is surrounded by five covered colonnades. Here a great number of disabled people used to lie—the blind, the lame, the paralyzed. One who was there had been an invalid for thirty-eight years. When Jesus saw him lying there and learned that he had been in this condition for a long time, he asked him, "Do you want to get well?" "Sir," the invalid replied, "I have no one to help me into the pool when the water is stirred. While I am trying to get in, someone else goes down ahead of me." Then Jesus said to him, "Get up! Pick up your mat and walk." At once the man was cured; he picked up his mat and walked. The day on which this took place was a Sabbath, and so the Jewish leaders said to the man who had been healed, "It is the Sabbath; the law forbids you to carry your mat." But he replied, "The man who made me well said to me, 'Pick up your mat and walk.' " So they asked him, "Who is this fellow who told you to pick it up and walk?" The man who was healed had no idea who it was, for Jesus had slipped away into the crowd that was there. Later Jesus found him at the temple and said to him, "See, you are well again. Stop sinning or something worse may happen to you." The man went away and told the Jewish leaders that it was Jesus who had made him well.

Focus on the Purity of our Hearts

When I was a young boy of about seven, I went to a school where many of the kids would make fun of me because of my small hand. They would call me small fingers at recess and I only had one friend to play with. My Mom eventually got me transferred to another school, as the teacher did not have control of the situation and I would come home crying a lot. I will never forget what she told me about my small hand. She said, "Joe, God has a special purpose for you in life, you and your small hand. One day, your small hand will be able to do a task no one else can. Maybe you will be able to reach into a small opening to get something out or who knows? But God made you just as he wants you, and those kids who are making fun of you are really making fun of God. They are going to be in trouble when they get to heaven." I went from being worried I was different to feeling special and important. My confidence was restored.

Just like the friend who played with me and my Mom, Jesus here has compassion on this man who had suffered for years. Who can we have compassion on today? When no one else would help him, Jesus did. He asks him an interesting question, "Do you want to get well?" At first we might react, "Of course he wants to get well." But I think Jesus here was not only referring to physical healing, but also to the healing of his soul. We will see later in the passage, Jesus warns him to stop sinning or something worse will happen to him. I believe he was talking about the condition of his heart. And as the teachers of the law were pressing him about who healed him on the Sabbath, he joined them in identifying Jesus, instead of challenging them as to why this mattered.

So today, when we wrestle with unfair illness, disability, and treatment, we know God cares and can heal us. Also know that he is a just God, and when we participate in worldly power grabs or attempts to be popular by fingering those who are doing good, God notices this too. Our hearts must be pure. We live in a world tight with the tension of many topics: political parties, people, and sin issues. We must focus on God's love and not the issues of the day. Only he can save us for eternity!

TAKEAWAYS

_____

_____

_____

_____

_____

Day 35

John 5:16-21

So, because Jesus was doing these things on the Sabbath, the Jewish leaders began to persecute him. In his defense Jesus said to them, "My Father is always at his work to this very day, and I too am working." For this reason they tried all the more to kill him; not only was he breaking the Sabbath, but he was even calling God his own Father, making himself equal with God. Jesus gave them this answer: "Very truly I tell you, the Son can do nothing by himself; he can do only what he sees his Father doing, because whatever the Father does the Son also does. For the Father loves the Son and shows him all he does. Yes, and he will show him even greater works than these, so that you will be amazed. For just as the Father raises the dead and gives them life, even so the Son gives life to whom he is pleased to give it.

<u>God's Work is Life</u>

Imagine a man who owned some land and he planned on developing it into a subdivision. One of his friends saw that he had hired a lot of people to level out the land but they were using pickup trucks with plows and scrapers. It was going to take a long time. He had a friend who owned a large tractor — an earth mover, designed to just do this work. His friend offered to lend the tractor to him. But this man was not willing to operate this tractor because the man was not "kosher" and did not eat the right food and so his tractor was considered unclean. This man's friend was trying to be kind and considerate, but he is labeled an outcast. And so this stubborn man lost out on saving months of work because he could not see God provision for him through this friend. In the same way, the Jewish leaders could not receive the "life" Jesus had for them, because they could not get past miracles on Sundays and the fact that he called God his Father. They saw him as a threat to their leadership and were going to find a technicality to pin on him. Instead of investigating whether Jesus was the Messiah, they simply wrote him off. Even more, they persecuted him and as his popularity grew, they tried to have him killed. Man-made conditions of faith never stand up or "hold water" compared to God's work in his servants on earth! We are his "hands and feet". He longs for us to be actively serving. When we are so in tune with God's heart that we can say whatever he does — we do; then we have become "Christ-like" and we have confidence to continue to operate amidst persecution. Then, we will SPREAD HIS LIGHT all around us and BREATHE the LIFE of God into the dry bones of those in this world.

I Peter 1:3-5 says this:

"Praise be to the God and Father of our Lord Jesus Christ! In his great mercy he has given us new birth into a living hope through the resurrection of Jesus Christ from the dead, and into an inheritance that can never perish, spoil or fade. This inheritance is kept in heaven for you, who through faith are shielded by God's power until the coming of the salvation that is ready to be revealed in the last time."

Let us be active in spreading the living hope of Jesus Christ today and every day, by the power of God! Such a great gift as Jesus Christ and his life cannot go to waste, it must be shared!

TAKEAWAYS

_____

_____

_____

_____

_____

Week 5 Top TAKEAWAYS

Look back at the past weeks devotionals and write down your top takeaways.

_____

_____

_____

_____

_____

Action/Implementation Steps

How do you plan to implement these take-aways in your life?

_____

_____

_____

_____

_____

Day 36

John 5:22-27

"Moreover, the Father judges no one, but has entrusted all judgment to the Son, that all may honor the Son just as they honor the Father. Whoever does not honor the Son does not honor the Father, who sent him. "Very truly I tell you, whoever hears my word and believes him who sent me has eternal life and will not be judged but has crossed over from death to life. Very truly I tell you, a time is coming and has now come when the dead will hear the voice of the Son of God and those who hear will live. For as the Father has life in himself, so he has granted the Son also to have life in himself. And he has given him authority to judge because he is the Son of Man."

A Trustworthy Judge

"Entrusted" is a key word here. The Father (God) entrusts all judgment to the Son (Jesus). This type of relationship is only built through faithfulness, trial, pain, and perseverance. Along with the entrusting responsibility comes TRANSFERRED HONOR. And this honor that is transferred from Father to Son should be honored by us. Not just because God the Father trusts the Son, but because of the Son's love, which is like the Father's love. True love requires judgment. Otherwise it is just pacifism. Many in our times (and in Jesus' times) will not take a stand for fear of offending or not being as popular with others. FEAR KILLS a movement because it squelches the belief of its members.

Isaiah 41:10 says, *"So do not fear, for I am with you; do not be dismayed, for I am your God. I will strengthen you and help you; I will uphold you with my righteous right hand."*

What people don't realize is that conviction-less faith will, in the end, condemn them. If judgment between right and wrong didn't matter, why would God grant the Son judgment power? As we will see later in this passage, it is clear that only the faithful of heart, those who follow Jesus and receive his gift, will inherit eternal life. Everyone else will be condemned. And while this is true, it is also true that those who follow Jesus wholeheartedly in life will experience HIS LIFE BREATHING into them. And those who follow this World will experience its death breathing into them. Three times Jesus says "Very Truly I tell you". He is trying to get our attention. This is called a "triple imperative", and it means it really important. You must trust and honor him to be his follower. Only true followers inherit eternal life. Do not trust in the world or the people or things of this world. You will be disappointed. They are fleeting. John 12:35, it says: *"Then Jesus told them, 'You are going to have the light just a little while longer. Walk in the light, before darkness overtakes you. Put your trust in the light while you still have it, so that you may become sons of light.'"*

Let us stay in the light of Christ and experience life — TRUE LIFE as we live!

TAKEAWAYS

_____

_____

_____

_____

_____

Day 37

John 5:28-30

[Jesus speaking] "Do not be amazed at this, for a time is coming when all who are in their graves will hear his voice and come out—those who have done what is good will rise to live, and those who have done what is evil will rise to be condemned. By myself I can do nothing; I judge only as I hear, and my judgment is just, for I seek not to please myself but him who sent me."

Humble and Confident

If someone were to ask you, "How would you define a Pure Heart?" What would you say? Many might tout off accomplishments, like giving large amounts of money or taking long pilgrimages, or feeding the hungry. It hit me in reading this passage that Jesus defines for us one of the most important aspects of a person with a pure heart towards God. It is found in the last verse above. "For I seek not to please myself but him who sent me." Out of this humility, and offering up of his will to God, Jesus served. And in serving in this way, he built a strong, powerful relationship with God- so strong that he was confident that whenever he acted in God's will, God would show up. And God was pleased with his Son and gave him authority to judge on his behalf.

This is something we can emulate about Jesus. He was the perfect model of submission to God. He only did God's will. As we roll into Christmas, celebrating Jesus' birth, let us focus only on what God's will is for our lives. How would he want us to spend our time, talent, and treasures? What does our Lord seek for us to do? Life is moving slow, but fast.

We live in deceptive times. There is a warning here as well — don't die without setting your heart right before God. I would hate to be awakened from the sleep of death only to find the agony of hell behind the door to the rest of my life.

We must fight for clarity in our relationship with God. Otherwise, we will get sucked up into the ways of the world.

TAKEAWAYS

_____

_____

_____

_____

_____

Day 38

John 5:31-35

[Jesus speaking] "If I testify about myself, my testimony is not true. There is another who testifies in my favor, and I know that his testimony about me is true. You have sent to John and he has testified to the truth. Not that I accept human testimony; but I mention it that you may be saved. John was a lamp that burned and gave light, and you chose for a time to enjoy his light."

The Search for The One

We are right now witnessing an incredible amount of people coming forward as eye witnesses to election irregularities and election fraud. This has the potential to be one of the most heavily contested elections in my lifetime. There are also eye witnesses who saw voting machines being tampered with, and even witnesses who have seen these same machines throw elections for one person over another, in other countries. There are now more than 1,000 sworn affidavits of eye witness testimony, under the penalty of perjury. If these stories all line up, this becomes extremely powerful proof of election irregularities and fraud. We have a media who likes the outcome of the election, and refuses to cover these eye witness testimonies. Eye witness testimony is considered to be evidence in a court of law. When a number of eye witnesses testify to the same thing happening, it becomes proof and believable. Why? Because it is very hard for many people to lie and also tell the exact same, detailed story, unless they really saw it.

In workers compensation, we sometimes have people who try and commit fraud. How do we prove they are not being truthful about an injury taking place in the workplace? We ask detailed questions at the time of the claim. Then later the adjuster asks detailed questions. If the two accounts do not match up, the person is lying.

Jesus was being accused of lying about his claims to be the Son of God, or the Messiah. So the teachers of the law and Pharisees asked him for proof. He acknowledges here that a person cannot be a witness for themselves. (But this is what the Pharisees did, they encouraged people to trust them because they were "the leaders". We hear these arguments today too.)

But Jesus reminds them that John the Baptist testified that he was coming. He called people to repentance to "make straight the path of the Lord." (John 1:23) Here is a summary of John's purpose in ministry, which he lived out. "He came as a witness to testify concerning the light, so that all men might believe. He himself was not the light; he came only as a witness to the light. The true light that gives light to every man was coming into the world." (John 1:6-8)

Why does Jesus tell these accusers this? He loves them and wants them to be saved. Can we love those who falsely accuse us? Can we pray for those who ridicule and persecute us? Jesus did.

John was a faithful servant of the King. He let God's light shine though him, and the Pharisees enjoyed its glow for a time. We must be faithful to shine our lights in any and every situation in life. COVID is not a good excuse to retreat and become self-focused. We must still serve and love, even amidst fear and restrictions. It is our calling. Jesus was preaching to "The One", he was searching for "The One" believer among many skeptics. He faced persecution to save "The One". Will we search for "The One" today?

TAKEAWAYS

_____

_____

_____

_____

_____

Day 39

John 5:36-47

(Jesus speaking) "I have testimony weightier than that of John. For the works that the Father has given me to finish— the very works that I am doing—testify that the Father has sent me. And the Father who sent me has himself testified concerning me. You have never heard his voice nor seen his form, nor does his word dwell in you, for you do not believe the one he sent. You study the Scriptures diligently because you think that in them you have eternal life. These are the very Scriptures that testify about me, yet you refuse to come to me to have life. I do not accept glory from human beings, but I know you. I know that you do not have the love of God in your hearts. I have come in my Father's name, and you do not accept me; but if someone else comes in his own name, you will accept him. How can you believe since you accept glory from one another but do not seek the glory that comes from the only God? But do not think I will accuse you before the Father. Your accuser is Moses, on whom your hopes are set. If you believed Moses, you would believe me, for he wrote about me. But since you do not believe what he wrote, how are you going to believe what I say?"

Aligned with God

If someone were to approach you and say, "My friend, Joe, here, he is a great baseball player" — would you believe them? Maybe. You might look at me and see if I look the part—I really don't. You might ask me a few questions about my background, my experience, and who my coaches were. Now if Ken Griffey Jr. (one of the highest vote-getters of all time entering the Baseball Hall of Fame) came up to you and said this, it would carry more weight. Furthermore, if you saw me making the same kind of plays Ken Griffey Jr. did (I know this is hard to believe, but I really can't) and hitting the baseball with the same authority, etc., then it would likely clinch this fact for you. You would be a believer.

Jesus is now going in for the kill, so to speak with the Pharisees. He has already presented evidence of his authority and position, that he was sent by God and is the Messiah. He did this with testimony from John. Now he presents three more evidences: 1) God testified about him, 2) Moses testified about him, and 3) The work he is doing is God's work.

How did God testify about him? He spoke out loud when Jesus was baptized by John the Baptist. "You are my Son whom I love; with you I am well pleased." (Luke 3:22)

How did Moses prophesy about Jesus? Let's look at Deuteronomy 18:15-19: "The Lord your God will raise up for you a prophet like me from among you, from your fellow Israelites. You must listen to him. For this is what you asked of the Lord your God at Horeb on the day of the assembly when you said, 'Let us not hear the voice of the Lord our God nor see this great fire anymore, or we will die.' The Lord said to me: 'What they say is good. I will raise up for them a prophet like you from among their fellow Israelites, and I will put my words in his mouth. He will tell them everything I command him. I myself will call to account anyone who does not listen to my words that the prophet speaks in my name.'"

This is likely the passage Jesus was referring to. Moses is also a representative of the prophets and the priests who prophesied about Jesus' coming all throughout the Old Testament.

And finally, we have his work. Jesus did incredible miracles — ones no one had ever seen before. Changing water into aged wine. Healing a man lame from birth, by just commanding him to stand up. Healing a child on their death bed with a word spoken at a huge distance. This work demonstrates the fact that he is ALIGNED WITH GOD — he is on God's team. In fact, it demonstrates he is God. If he was not God, as he claimed to be, God would not have given him the power to act like himself.

This brings us to a point of application ... what evidence is there that I am FROM God and ALIGNED WITH God? Are there people who serve alongside me that can testify to this? God does give me power to love, serve, and heal while I am doing his work. Are there ways I have followed God that blow people's minds?

This is the model that Jesus gave to us. It is the model we are privileged to follow. Let's join together and transform this broken world one soul at a time!

TAKEAWAYS

_____

_____

_____

_____

_____

Day 40

John 6:1-9

Some time after this, Jesus crossed to the far shore of the Sea of Galilee (that is, the Sea of Tiberias), and a great crowd of people followed him because they saw the signs he had performed by healing the sick. Then Jesus went up on a mountainside and sat down with his disciples. The Jewish Passover Festival was near. When Jesus looked up and saw a great crowd coming toward him, he said to Philip, "Where shall we buy bread for these people to eat?" He asked this only to test him, for he already had in mind what he was going to do. Philip answered him, "It would take more than half a year's wages to buy enough bread for each one to have a bite!" Another of his disciples, Andrew, Simon Peter's brother, spoke up, "Here is a boy with five small barley loaves and two small fish, but how far will they go among so many?"

Faith Tested

A little bit of time had passed since Jesus was in Jerusalem, and he and his disciples had traveled 60-70 miles to the Sea of Galilee. This miracle appears in all four gospels and it allows us to see (by referencing through the four gospels) why these people followed Jesus. After his baptism by John the Baptist, and the temptation of Jesus, which happened in the desert between Jerusalem and the Dead Sea (or the Salt Sea), we find many stories throughout the four gospels about Jesus' miracles. Matthew 4:23-24 summarizes this time of ministry this way: "Jesus went throughout Galilee, teaching in their synagogues, preaching the good news of the kingdom, and healing every kind of disease and sickness among the people. News about him spread all over Syria [just north of the Sea of Galilee], and people brought to him all who were ill with various diseases, those suffering severe pain, the demon possessed, those having seizures, and the paralyzed, and he healed them." On your own time you can scan through each gospel and get a small sampling of these miracles. The point is, Jesus was HEALING people frequently, for a long period of time. No one had ever or has ever (in recorded history) seen such an incredible display of dominion and power over this life! He breathed life literally into all he was around; either physically, spiritually, or both. And this sets the stage for The Feeding of the 5,000. No wonder so many followed him. His daily miracles were compelling, and it was surreal and mind-blowing for the people.

And so we find that Jesus is always teaching and investing in his disciples. He tests Phillip here. He wants to see if he truly gets the fact that he is God — that he is all-powerful. Phillip's mind jumps to the sheer impossibility of it all — "eight months wages would not buy enough bread". This is a typical human response. Many respond this way to this day. I do sometimes. Then Andrew gets resourceful, and finds what they do have to work with — five loaves and two fishes. By the way, it wasn't just 5000 people — that was just the men. It was likely 10,000 to 15,000 people in total, including the women and children. So this begs the question of us: Do I truly believe Jesus is all-powerful, that he is the Son of God? Or will I get caught up in the impossibility of it all? Andrew set for me a good model here to follow, he found what supplies they had and offered them up.

In life today, some decisions, situations, and challenges seem out of my reach to solve or fix. I can either throw up my hands and give up, or I can offer up to Jesus what I have and see what he will make of my meager offerings! It is all a matter of how big of a God I perceive is with me and how powerful I believe Jesus is to save. Perspective is key! So today, I can look at the challenges before me, call out in earnest prayer to God, and see him work mightily in my midst on a daily and weekly basis. I just have to believe and actively look to join him in his work. Life, TRUE LIFE, is found in Jesus Christ!

TAKEAWAYS

_____

_____

_____

_____

_____

Day 41

John 6:10-15

Jesus said, "Have the people sit down." There was plenty of grass in that place, and they sat down (about five thousand men were there). Jesus then took the loaves, gave thanks, and distributed to those who were seated as much as they wanted. He did the same with the fish. When they had all had enough to eat, he said to his disciples, "Gather the pieces that are left over. Let nothing be wasted." So they gathered them and filled twelve baskets with the pieces of the five barley loaves left over by those who had eaten. After the people saw the sign Jesus performed, they began to say, "Surely this is the Prophet who is to come into the world." Jesus, knowing that they intended to come and make him king by force, withdrew again to a mountain by himself.

Fame or Faithfulness

I have had clients who have been with me for a long time. They have seen hard work and savings, while at other times they have found it challenging to be my client. Other clients will leave on a dime, whenever a challenge presents itself. Why have the loyal clients stuck with me over the good and bad times? I like to think it is not because I am always the cheapest price or the most popular option. I find they trust me to act in their best interest. They believe I have their best in mind. They see my heart and realize that I will be an honest and true fiduciary of their business interests.

Jesus searched for those who would be true followers. He is an honest and true fiduciary of the interests of our hearts! He performs the miracle here of multiplying the loaves and the fishes, and we have several take-aways:

1) The multiplication of what is given. When we give to or join in the Lord's work, out of a heart set on his ways and his kingdom, he will MULTIPLY THE RESULTS. This truth is perhaps best displayed in John 4:35: "Do you not say, 'Four months more and then the harvest? I tell you, open your eyes and look at the fields! They are ripe for harvest." Verse 38 says, "I sent you to reap what you have not worked for. Others have done the hard work, and you have reaped the benefits of their labor."

2) The people only believed because of the miracles. They were Conditional Believers. They only followed Jesus because they wanted to make him king (for what they wanted out of him). This is why Jesus said they intended to make him king by force. This was not why he was here.

3) Jesus stayed on mission, though it was likely very tempting to get swept up in all the fame and popularity. He was not there to be a king on earth. He came to sacrifice all to eternally save us all as the King of Kings and Lord of All!

So we have some questions to consider today. 1) Will we be faithful, like the little boy, to give our relatively meager offerings to God of our time, talent, and treasures — so he can multiply their impact? 2) Will we be Conditional Believers or will we choose to follow loyally, in the good and the bad times, after Jesus Christ? 3) Will we seek to know God's heart and stay on mission to what he has called us to be in this world (as evidenced in his Word) — HIS AMBASSADORS?

TAKEAWAYS

_____

_____

_____

_____

Day 42
John 6:16-21

When evening came, his disciples went down to the lake, where they got into a boat and set off across the lake for Capernaum. By now it was dark, and Jesus had not yet joined them. A strong wind was blowing and the waters grew rough. When they had rowed about three or four miles, they saw Jesus approaching the boat, walking on the water; and they were frightened. But he said to them, "It is I; DON'T BE AFRAID." Then they were willing to take him into the boat, and immediately the boat reached the shore where they were heading.

Two Types of Fear

The disciples were likely already afraid of the storm that beset them. Darkness and high winds can easily create a panic and fearful tendencies. Then "a ghost" walking on the water probably put them over the edge. FEAR CAN CRIPPLE people and cause them to give up. Have you seen fear in our cities, in our leaders in our nation these days? I have. In the moment, fear can be good — like being afraid of a fire and running from it. Overall though, "fear of the unknown", or forces or things we have no control over — like when we will die — is destructive and disabling.

1 John 4:18 say this: "There is no fear in love. But PERFECT LOVE DRIVES OUT FEAR, because fear has to do with punishment. The one who fears is not made perfect in love."

So what does it look like to live a life free from this terrifying fear we can experience?

Well, to do this, we must engage another type of fear — the Fear of The Lord. Psalm 111:10 says, "The fear of the

Lord is the beginning of wisdom; all who follow his precepts have good understanding. To him be eternal praise." Wisdom and understanding are universally sought after by us all, right? In another part of the Bible, Jesus is warning his disciples about fearing the Pharisees and what they could do to them. He says, "I tell you, my friends, do not be afraid of those who kill the body and after that can do no more. But I will show you whom you should fear: Fear him who, after the killing of the body, has the power to throw you into hell. Yes, I tell you, fear him." (Luke 12:4-5)

So, we see that we are to fear God instead of man. But this is a different type of fear. We do not need to be afraid of God, because he is perfect in love. So how do we fear him? This type of fear is referencing extreme honor and respect. It is this recognition of his power to save and to help us, that motivates us to follow him and take risks within his will. The fear of God removes the fears of this world. This fear is one we CLING TO; it is reverence and recognition of His ultimate power. It might be compared to the fear a child has of their father. They know he is good. They also know that a good father disciplines their children and deserves respect. The disciples were fearful of forces they had no control over. They found that Jesus did possess this control. By performing this miracle of "the boat automatically reaching shore", Jesus reinforced to them they should fear God and fear him. Today, what is it that you fear? Is it helping you accomplish your life mission in Christ Jesus? Let us fear the Lord and HIM ONLY!

TAKEAWAYS

Week 6 Top TAKEAWAYS

Look back at the past weeks devotionals and write down your top takeaways.

_____

_____

_____

_____

_____

Action/Implementation Steps

How do you plan to implement these take-aways in your life?

_____

_____

_____

_____

_____

Day 43

John 6:22-29

The next day the crowd that had stayed on the op-posite shore of the lake realized that only one boat had been there, and that Jesus had not entered it with his disciples, but that they had gone away alone. Then some boats from Tiberias landed near the place where the people had eaten the bread after the Lord had giv-en thanks. Once the crowd realized that neither Jesus nor his disciples were there, they got into the boats and went to Capernaum in search of Jesus. When they found him on the other side of the lake, they asked him, "Rab-bi, when did you get here?" Jesus answered, "Very truly I tell you, you are looking for me, not because you saw the signs I performed but because you ate the loaves and had your fill. Do not work for food that spoils, but for food that endures to eternal life, which the Son of Man will give you. For on him God the Father has placed his seal of approval." Then they asked him, "What must we do to do the works God requires?" Jesus answered, "The work of God is this: to believe in the one he has sent."

Power Through With the Word

Why do we search for God? What is it we desire from him? I grew up in a church that taught "the pursuit of God" as trying really hard to not do the wrong things. This sounds noble, but in the end is an empty way to live. It is life fo-cused on the negative and a life lived in comparison to oth-ers. These followers of Jesus had lived with this model from the Pharisees for some time. Now Jesus came and preached a different way to live and did miracles and even fed them. It is almost like they were so hungry for the moment that changed their thinking, they wanted that moment over and over again. They wanted the perpetual "Mountaintop Experience"! Many live life this way today. They live for the extreme and plan for the next bucket list item. This too becomes empty over time. Here Jesus encourages them to seek after "food" that will last to eternal life. Jesus is an overflowing supply of this food, because he devotes himself to the Word of God — in fact, he is the Word of God. John 1:1 tells us: "In the beginning was the Word, and the Word was with God, and the Word was God." (It goes on to equate The Word to Jesus.) So we can try hard on our own strength to do God's work, but we will fail. Or, we can believe in the one he has sent, Jesus Christ, and digest his spiritual body and live. When we dig into God's Word (Jesus) and we apply it to our lives, we have connected OUR PASSION TO GOD'S POWER source and we live a life fulfilled no matter the current circumstances. Is life challenging or hard today? Do you feel isolated and/or beat down? I do sometimes. Let's power through with The Word!

TAKEAWAYS

_____

_____

_____

_____

_____

Day 44

John 6:30-35

So they asked him, "What sign then will you give that we may see it and believe you? What will you do? Our ancestors ate the manna in the wilderness; as it is written: 'He gave them bread from heaven to eat.' " Jesus said to them, "Very truly I tell you, it is not Moses who has given you the bread from heaven, but it is my Father who gives you the true bread from heaven. For the bread of God is the bread that comes down from heaven and gives life to the world." "Sir," they said, "always give us this bread." Then Jesus declared, "I am the bread of life. Whoever comes to me will never go hungry, and whoever believes in me will never be thirsty."

A Nourished Life

When we are in the middle of God's work, full of his Spirit, he sustains us! Here we have the crowd continuing to want their collective bellies fed, missing the point. It must have seemed strange to have a homeless wanderer of a teacher, who likely went hungry from time to time, say this. How could he be the source of unending bread? Well, sure, he did just multiply the bread and fish for them — there is that. So we see Jesus again painting a picture of spiritual life through a physical analogy. Bread only sustains us for a short period of time. Water is even shorter. God provides the sun and the rain for the harvest of wheat. He proves the water for drink. He is behind all that grows on this earth. He also specifically provided the Manna from heaven they are referring to here. So it is not surprising that he also is completely behind our spiritual nourishment and spiritual life. We live by eating bread and drinking water. Jesus and his way of life is what we are to seek, develop, and act on in our lives. THIS FOCUS is what FEEDS our good works and makes them acceptable to God. Receive the truth of the Word of God and live a nourished life!

TAKEAWAYS

_____

_____

_____

_____

_____

Day 45

John 6:36-40

[Jesus speaking]

"But as I told you, you have seen me and still you do not believe. All those the Father gives me will come to me, and whoever comes to me I will never drive away. For I have come down from heaven not to do my will, but to do the will of him who sent me. And this is the will of him who sent me, that I shall lose none of all those he has given me, but raise them up at the last day. For my Father's will is that everyone who looks to the Son and believes in him shall have eternal life, and I will raise them up at the last day."

<u>Live Richly</u>

Jesus was not just "others-focused", he was God-focused. We cannot truly be others-focused with a sinful, selfish heart. Only God can change our hearts. So, when we are God-focused, we are others focused too. Jesus made his daily plans based on who God is and how he is working around him. He was not worried about what others thought about him, nor did he spend time, energy, or talent trying to win their approval. He was singularly focused on who God the Father was drawing to him.

As we read further into this passage, we see that Jesus understood the concept of God entrusting others to his care. Similar to how a foster parent might volunteer to take children under their care, Jesus has signed up to care for you and me. We just have to look to him in life and FOLLOW HIS LEAD. He is committed to keeping us in his spiritual fold. He is the Good Shepherd! John 10:11 says, "I am the

GOOD SHEPHERD. The GOOD SHEPHERD lays down his life for his sheep." Yesterday, today, and tomorrow Jesus is laying down his life for you and me. God is actively drawing others to himself. We are his ambassadors in this world. So we get to come alongside others being drawn by God, and train them to look to Jesus rapidly and often in this sinful world. In the end, he will raise us up and we will get recognized with him in glory! So what we sacrifice today in recognition and fame, in fair treatment and justice, will pale in comparison to all that we gain today and will gain following Jesus. Let's follow this Good Shepherd who feeds us and LIVE RICHLY in his wonderful grace!

TAKEAWAYS

Day 46

John 6:41-51

At this the Jews there began to grumble about him because he said, "I am the bread that came down from heaven." They said, "Is this not Jesus, the son of Joseph, whose father and mother we know? How can he now say, 'I came down from heaven'?" "Stop grumbling among yourselves," Jesus answered. "No one can come to me unless the Father who sent me draws them, and I will raise them up at the last day. It is written in the Prophets: 'They will all be taught by God.' Everyone who has heard the Father and learned from him comes to me. No one has seen the Father except the one who is from God; only he has seen the Father. Very truly I tell you, the one who believes has eternal life. I am the bread of life. Your ancestors ate the manna in the wilderness, yet they died. But here is the bread that comes down from heaven, which anyone may eat and not die. I am the living bread that came down from heaven. Whoever eats this bread will live forever. This bread is my flesh, which I will give for the life of the world."

A Christmas Message — Greater Hope

The Old Testament prophet Isaiah foretold a better future for the Jews. He saw in the midst of turmoil and hardship a much grander place, a much larger and more successful people! Isaiah 54:2-5 says this: ""Sing, barren woman, you who never bore a child; burst into song, shout for joy, you who were never in labor; because more are the children of the desolate woman than of her who has a husband," says the Lord. "Enlarge the place of your tent, stretch your tent curtains wide, do not hold back; lengthen your cords, strengthen your stakes. For you will spread out to the right and to the left; your descendants will dispossess nations and settle in their desolate cities. Do not be afraid; you will not be put to shame. Do not fear disgrace; you will not be humiliated. You will forget the shame of your youth and remember no more the reproach of your widowhood. For your Maker is your husband— the Lord Almighty is his name— the Holy One of Israel is your Redeemer; he is called the God of all the earth." (Isaiah 54:2-5) Later on in this chapter, we find the section quoted here by Jesus in John 6, "All your sons will be taught by the Lord, and great will be your children's peace. In righteousness you will be established: Tyranny will be far from you; you will have nothing to fear."

Christians in the US are living in a great time of uncertainty (now we can better empathize with Christians around the world.) In the past, the IRS, the FBI, and other groups were to some degree weaponized against those of a certain political party or belief system. Now we have Cancel Culture, Woke Mindset, and massive political divides in our country. Some are defunding the police, blaming them as a group for the problems of a few, and creating lawless zones. Greed and corruption is rampant. Free speech is suppressed. We are seeing the results of a generational shift away from the Christian principles our country was founded on. It can be very scary and hard to deal with. The Jews experienced this, as well. They had fallen away, over and over again, from God and his ways, and gotten mixed up in ways of their pagan neighbors. Then God allowed judgment in the form of captivity, over and over again. But Isaiah in the Old Testament foresaw a time of healing. He saw past their current circumstances to a time that would TRANSFORM THE DEFINITION of success for the Jews. It was the birth, life, death, and resurrection of Jesus Christ—that which we celebrate on Christmas. He tells them they need to "enlarge the place of your tent", "widen your tent curtains", and "lengthen your cords, strengthen your stakes." This means to prepare for more ... for things much bigger ... for success beyond their wildest dreams. All of this language, over and over again, tells them that it is very, very important that they LOOK DEEP and TRULY SEE their bright future! I can only imagine how many Jews over the years read this section of Isaiah and wished it was happening right at the time they read it, while they were in captivity.

We live in a world CAPTIVE to sin, my friends. We see it all around us -- the chains of sin that weigh people down, yoke them to destructive ways, and rob them of their joy and hope. Jesus in this section was telling his Jewish brothers and sisters that, thought they persecuted him, he loved them and was the one sent to rescue them from their sinful ways and usher in the time period of new TRANSFORMATIONAL SUCCESS! He is the living bread; he sustains our spirits with hope for eternity. He is building us up — exercising our bodies, equipping us for success in eternity. By quoting this simple, likely well-known phrase from Isaiah, "They will all be taught by God", he recalls in the minds of every devout Jew this great promise of a new and wildly successful kingdom.

Today, when you see the challenges, when you're crying over the injustices, when you are hurt by things stolen from you, place your mind in Jesus' hands. LISTEN to his words of hope. "I am the living bread that came down from heaven. If anyone eats of this bread, he will live forever. This bread is my flesh, which I will give for the life of the world." Jesus gave us living bread to experience heaven, in part, here on earth. We can have great hope today in Jesus and his power to save. And we have GREATER HOPE tomorrow in our eternal significance in heaven! Rejoice and be glad! Great is our reward! We are chosen and equipped to do the good works God has prepared in advance for us to do through the Bread of Life — Jesus Christ. Breathe deeply of his strength and humbly rely on his POWER TO SAVE!

TAKEAWAYS

_____

_____

_____

_____

_____

Day 47
John 6:52-58

[Jesus speaking]

"Then the Jews began to argue sharply among them-selves, "How can this man give us his flesh to eat?" Jesus said to them, "Very truly I tell you, unless you eat the flesh of the Son of Man and drink his blood, you have no life in you. Whoever eats my flesh and drinks my blood has eternal life, and I will raise them up at the last day. For my flesh is real food and my blood is real drink. Whoever eats my flesh and drinks my blood remains in me, and I in them. Just as the living Father sent me and I live because of the Father, so the one who feeds on me will live because of me. This is the bread that came down from heaven. Your ancestors ate manna and died, but whoever feeds on this bread will live forever."

<u>Digesting Jesus ... It's a Life Changer</u>

Blood makes the heart beat. Flesh is part of the basic structure of an operating body. Jesus is clearly not talking in actual terms here, but figuratively and spiritually. When we have high respect for someone and their influence on us (the model of living a good life) we try to emulate them, or do what they did. We — out of respect, appreciation, and a recognition that what they did had weight in life — will follow in their footsteps.

I have tried to do this with my Mom. She died when she was 48, and I was 14. It was very tough to lose her. It still is, especially around Christmas. However, in remembering her and the weight of her life, I have tried to take a few things she did and emulate them — incorporate them into my life. I have had a lot of time to think about "what made my Mom's heart beat" (like blood pumping)? What was "core" to her body of work in life (like flesh)? A couple of the majors come to mind. 1) She reached out and cared for people in special ways in the moment. She would listen to their hearts and try and see what really mattered to them. She would show them they had "high value" in her eyes. 2) She was excellent in the way she performed her love; nothing was too lavish. For birthdays, she made amazing castle cakes, and for church she practiced and practiced singing her duets. When she went to teach ESL to refugees, she also had her standards — she went to their homes and taught them from the Bible. She even did this in a wheelchair during cancer treatments.

I think of this as I read this passage, because when you get beyond that odd physical reaction to eating flesh and drinking blood and dig into what he is saying — it is powerful. Jesus is saying he is the source of a NEW LIFE here on earth and one that will last forever. He is the Messiah who will lead the way for us. It is not good enough to watch him in "awe" and admire his ways. It is not good enough to intellectually agree with him. TO GAIN THIS LIFE, WE MUST LIVE IT! To live it well, we must figure out what moves his heart and what was core to his success in life. We must drink of his blood and eat his flesh. We must feed spiritually on it every day and have it penetrate into our wicked hearts to redeem us!

Oh, Jesus the Christ, here is my open heart, broken with sin and selfishness! I offer it up and ask you to pump your blood in and rebuild your flesh into my body. Do this so I can be free to love and serve as you did. May I be healed by your everlasting life so I can be a BEACON OF LIGHT in a dark and hurting world!

TAKEAWAYS

_____

_____

_____

_____

_____

Day 48

John 6:59-71

He said this while teaching in the synagogue in Capernaum. On hearing it, many of his disciples said, "This is a hard teaching. Who can accept it?" Aware that his disciples were grumbling about this, Jesus said to them, "Does this offend you? Then what if you see the Son of Man ascend to where he was before! The Spirit gives life; the flesh counts for nothing. The words I have spoken to you—they are full of the Spirit and life. Yet there are some of you who do not believe." For Jesus had known from the beginning which of them did not believe and who would betray him. He went on to say, "This is why I told you that no one can come to me unless the Father has enabled them." From this time many of his disciples turned back and no longer followed him. "You do not want to leave too, do you?" Jesus asked the Twelve. Simon Peter answered him, "Lord, to whom shall we go? You have the words of eternal life. We have come to believe and to know that you are the Holy One of God." Then Jesus replied, "Have I not chosen you, the Twelve? Yet one of you is a devil!" (He meant Judas, the son of Simon Iscariot, who, though one of the Twelve, was later to betray him.)

Following Jesus When It's Not Popular

To Jesus, it was important he was clear with his disciples. He looked for those whom his Father had enabled to believe. Those who chose to leave behind the ways of the world and follow him with undivided devotion. He is still looking for these true followers today.

After performing all of his miracles, he was the most popular person in the region. Crowds swarmed to him and they wanted to make him king by force. This was definitely a "Mountaintop Experience"! But this was not the mountaintop Jesus was aiming for. He was not searching to become the most popular, he was on a different mission. He desired to follow God's will. And God's will required him to preach the truth and eventually be tortured and sacrifice his life for all of mankind. This meant instead of dwelling on his popularity status, he must keep climbing. After this tough teaching, many of his disciples left. They decided following wasn't fun anymore.

So many times in life, we humans tend to pay attention to the size of the crowd and their praise. This can be so deceptive, as the heart of man is corrupted by sin. The few who followed the truth for the right reasons had done the heartwork to digest Jesus and had committed their lives to him. Simon Peter is a good example of this. When asked by Jesus: "You do not want to leave too, do you?" Peter says, "Where shall we go? You have the words of eternal life. We believe and know that you are the Holy One of God."

Peter expresses a faith that was rooted deeper ... deeper than the popular winds of the day could blow over! How am I seeking to know Jesus and build deeper roots today? How do I help my family and those around me build the deeper roots of faith in their lives? In the end, it is the Spirit that gives life; all that is accomplished in the flesh counts for nothing.

TAKEAWAYS

_____

_____

_____

_____

Week 7 Top TAKEAWAYS

Look back at the past weeks devotionals and write down your top takeaways.

_____

_____

_____

_____

_____

Action/Implementation Steps

How do you plan to implement these take-aways in your life?

_____

_____

_____

_____

Top Action Steps Implemented

1-_____

_____

2-_____

_____

3-_____

_____

4-_____

_____

<u>Recognitions:</u>

I want to specifically thank Cherish Anderson and Kathy Wilson, my editors; Robert Sweesy my publisher; and Christina Sweesy, the graphic designer for this book.

Big shoutouts go to my friends Todd Grande and Tom Skeie for encouraging me to write devotionals, Don Anderson and the Thursday group for all of your support, and my church, Rockharbor, for filling my mind with truth, and creating a community of believers that support me. Finally, to my family and friends who have read and/or commented on my devotionals to help me improve, I am blessed by you. And most of all, to my Lord and Savior Jesus Christ – whose Spirit has propelled me in an impact in life way beyond my abilities.

REAL TIME DEVOTIONALS

www.ingramcontent.com/pod-product-compliance
Lightning Source LLC
Chambersburg PA
CBHW051429090426
42737CB00014B/2888